CS-37   GENERAL APTITUDE AND ABILITIES SERIES

This is your
PASSBOOK for...

Preparing Written Material

Test Preparation Study Guide
Questions & Answers

COPYRIGHT NOTICE

This book is SOLELY intended for, is sold ONLY to, and its use is RESTRICTED to individual, bona fide applicants or candidates who qualify by virtue of having seriously filed applications for appropriate license, certificate, professional and/or promotional advancement, higher school matriculation, scholarship, or other legitimate requirements of education and/or governmental authorities.

This book is NOT intended for use, class instruction, tutoring, training, duplication, copying, reprinting, excerption, or adaptation, etc., by:

1) Other publishers
2) Proprietors and/or Instructors of "Coaching" and/or Preparatory Courses
3) Personnel and/or Training Divisions of commercial, industrial, and governmental organizations
4) Schools, colleges, or universities and/or their departments and staffs, including teachers and other personnel
5) Testing Agencies or Bureaus
6) Study groups which seek by the purchase of a single volume to copy and/or duplicate and/or adapt this material for use by the group as a whole without having purchased individual volumes for each of the members of the group
7) Et al.

Such persons would be in violation of appropriate Federal and State statutes.

PROVISION OF LICENSING AGREEMENTS – Recognized educational, commercial, industrial, and governmental institutions and organizations, and others legitimately engaged in educational pursuits, including training, testing, and measurement activities, may address request for a licensing agreement to the copyright owners, who will determine whether, and under what conditions, including fees and charges, the materials in this book may be used them. In other words, a licensing facility exists for the legitimate use of the material in this book on other than an individual basis. However, it is asseverated and affirmed here that the material in this book CANNOT be used without the receipt of the express permission of such a licensing agreement from the Publishers. Inquiries re licensing should be addressed to the company, attention rights and permissions department.

All rights reserved, including the right of reproduction in whole or in part, in any form or by any means, electronic or mechanical, including photocopying, recording, or by any information storage and retrieval system, without permission in writing from the Publisher.

Copyright © 2024 by
National Learning Corporation

212 Michael Drive, Syosset, NY 11791
(516) 921-8888 • www.passbooks.com
E-mail: info@passbooks.com

PUBLISHED IN THE UNITED STATES OF AMERICA

PASSBOOK® SERIES

THE *PASSBOOK® SERIES* has been created to prepare applicants and candidates for the ultimate academic battlefield – the examination room.

At some time in our lives, each and every one of us may be required to take an examination – for validation, matriculation, admission, qualification, registration, certification, or licensure.

Based on the assumption that every applicant or candidate has met the basic formal educational standards, has taken the required number of courses, and read the necessary texts, the *PASSBOOK® SERIES* furnishes the one special preparation which may assure passing with confidence, instead of failing with insecurity. Examination questions – together with answers – are furnished as the basic vehicle for study so that the mysteries of the examination and its compounding difficulties may be eliminated or diminished by a sure method.

This book is meant to help you pass your examination provided that you qualify and are serious in your objective.

The entire field is reviewed through the huge store of content information which is succinctly presented through a provocative and challenging approach – the question-and-answer method.

A climate of success is established by furnishing the correct answers at the end of each test.

You soon learn to recognize types of questions, forms of questions, and patterns of questioning. You may even begin to anticipate expected outcomes.

You perceive that many questions are repeated or adapted so that you can gain acute insights, which may enable you to score many sure points.

You learn how to confront new questions, or types of questions, and to attack them confidently and work out the correct answers.

You note objectives and emphases, and recognize pitfalls and dangers, so that you may make positive educational adjustments.

Moreover, you are kept fully informed in relation to new concepts, methods, practices, and directions in the field.

You discover that you are actually taking the examination all the time: you are preparing for the examination by "taking" an examination, not by reading extraneous and/or supererogatory textbooks.

In short, this PASSBOOK®, used directedly, should be an important factor in helping you to pass your test.

PREPARING WRITTEN MATERIAL

INTRODUCTION

These questions test for the ability to present information clearly and accurately, and to organize paragraphs logically and comprehensibly. For some questions, you will be given information in two or three sentences followed by four restatements of the information. You must then choose the best version. For other questions, you will be given paragraphs with their sentences out of order. You must then choose, from four suggestions, the BEST order for the sentences. There will be 15 questions in this subject on the written test.

Test Task: There are two separate test tasks in this subject area.

- For the first, Information Presentation, you will be given information in two or three sentences, followed by four restatements of the information. You must then choose the best version.

- For the second, Paragraph Organization, you will be given paragraphs with their sentences out of order, and then be asked to choose, from among four suggestions, the best order for the sentences. There will be five Paragraph Organization questions on the written test.

Information Presentation

1. Martin Wilson failed to take proper precautions. His failure to take proper precautions caused a personal injury accident.
   Which one of the following BEST presents the information above?
   A. Martin Wilson failed to take proper precautions that caused a personal injury accident.
   B. Proper precautions, which Martin Wilson failed to take, caused a personal injury accident.
   C. Martin Wilson's failure to take proper precautions caused a personal injury accident.
   D. Martin Wilson, who failed to take proper precautions, was in a personal injury accident.

1.____

Paragraph Organization

The following question is based upon a group of sentences. The sentences are shown out of sequence, but when correctly arranged, they form a connected, well-organize paragraph. Read the sentences, and then answer the question about the best arrangement of these sentences.

2.
I. Eventually, they piece all of this information together and make a choice.
II. Before actually deciding upon a job in nutrition services, people usually think about several possibilities.
III. They imagine themselves in different situations, and in so doing, they probably think about their interests, goals, and abilities.
IV. Choosing an occupation in the field of nutrition services is an important decision to make.

Which one of the following is the BEST arrangement of these sentences?
A. II, IV, I, III   B. II, III, IV, I   C. IV, II, I, III   D. IV, II, III, I

2.____

KEY (CORRECT ANSWERS)

1. The correct answer is C.
Choice A conveys the incorrect impression that proper precautions caused a personal injury accident.
Choice B conveys the incorrect impression that proper precautions caused a personal injury accident.
Choice C best presents the original information: Martin Wilson failed to take proper precautions and this failure caused a personal injury accident.
Choice D states that Martin Wilson was in a personal injury accident. The original information states that Martin Wilson caused a personal injury accident, but it does not state that Martin Wilson was in a personal injury accident.

2. The correct answer is D.
Choices A and C present the information in the paragraph out of logical sequence. In both A and C, sentence I comes before sentence III. The key element in the organization of this paragraph is that sentence III contains the information to which sentence I refers; therefore, in logical sequence, sentence III should come before sentence I.
Choice B also presents the information in the paragraph out of logical sequence. Choice B places sentence IV in between sentence I and sentence III, thereby interrupting the logical sequence of the information in the paragraph.
Choice D presents the information in the paragraph in the best logical sequence. Sentence IV introduces the main idea of the paragraph: "choosing an occupation in the field of nutrition services." Sentences II, III, I then follow up on this idea by describing, in order, the steps involved in making such a choice. Choice D is the best answer to this sample question.

HOW TO TAKE A TEST

You have studied long, hard and conscientiously.

With your official admission card in hand, and your heart pounding, you have been admitted to the examination room.

You note that there are several hundred other applicants in the examination room waiting to take the same test.

They all appear to be equally well prepared.

You know that nothing but your best effort will suffice. The "moment of truth" is at hand: you now have to demonstrate objectively, in writing, your knowledge of content and your understanding of subject matter.

You are fighting the most important battle of your life—to pass and/or score high on an examination which will determine your career and provide the economic basis for your livelihood.

What extra, special things should you know and should you do in taking the examination?

I. YOU MUST PASS AN EXAMINATION

A. WHAT EVERY CANDIDATE SHOULD KNOW
Examination applicants often ask us for help in preparing for the written test. What can I study in advance? What kinds of questions will be asked? How will the test be given? How will the papers be graded?

B. HOW ARE EXAMS DEVELOPED?
Examinations are carefully written by trained technicians who are specialists in the field known as "psychological measurement," in consultation with recognized authorities in the field of work that the test will cover. These experts recommend the subject matter areas or skills to be tested; only those knowledges or skills important to your success on the job are included. The most reliable books and source materials available are used as references. Together, the experts and technicians judge the difficulty level of the questions.
Test technicians know how to phrase questions so that the problem is clearly stated. Their ethics do not permit "trick" or "catch" questions. Questions may have been tried out on sample groups, or subjected to statistical analysis, to determine their usefulness.
Written tests are often used in combination with performance tests, ratings of training and experience, and oral interviews. All of these measures combine to form the best-known means of finding the right person for the right job.

II. HOW TO PASS THE WRITTEN TEST

A. BASIC STEPS

1) Study the announcement

How, then, can you know what subjects to study? Our best answer is: "Learn as much as possible about the class of positions for which you've applied." The exam will test the knowledge, skills and abilities needed to do the work.

Your most valuable source of information about the position you want is the official exam announcement. This announcement lists the training and experience qualifications. Check these standards and apply only if you come reasonably close to meeting them. Many jurisdictions preview the written test in the exam announcement by including a section called "Knowledge and Abilities Required," "Scope of the Examination," or some similar heading. Here you will find out specifically what fields will be tested.

2) Choose appropriate study materials

If the position for which you are applying is technical or advanced, you will read more advanced, specialized material. If you are already familiar with the basic principles of your field, elementary textbooks would waste your time. Concentrate on advanced textbooks and technical periodicals. Think through the concepts and review difficult problems in your field.

These are all general sources. You can get more ideas on your own initiative, following these leads. For example, training manuals and publications of the government agency which employs workers in your field can be useful, particularly for technical and professional positions. A letter or visit to the government department involved may result in more specific study suggestions, and certainly will provide you with a more definite idea of the exact nature of the position you are seeking.

3) Study this book!

III. KINDS OF TESTS

Tests are used for purposes other than measuring knowledge and ability to perform specified duties. For some positions, it is equally important to test ability to make adjustments to new situations or to profit from training. In others, basic mental abilities not dependent on information are essential. Questions which test these things may not appear as pertinent to the duties of the position as those which test for knowledge and information. Yet they are often highly important parts of a fair examination. For very general questions, it is almost impossible to help you direct your study efforts. What we can do is to point out some of the more common of these general abilities needed in public service positions and describe some typical questions.

1) General information

Broad, general information has been found useful for predicting job success in some kinds of work. This is tested in a variety of ways, from vocabulary lists to questions about current events. Basic background in some field of work, such as sociology or economics, may be sampled in a group of questions. Often these are principles which have become familiar to most persons through exposure rather than through formal training. It is difficult to advise you how to study for these questions; being alert to the world around you is our best suggestion.

2) Verbal ability

An example of an ability needed in many positions is verbal or language ability. Verbal ability is, in brief, the ability to use and understand words. Vocabulary and grammar tests are typical measures of this ability. Reading comprehension or paragraph interpretation questions are common in many kinds of civil service tests. You are given a paragraph of written material and asked to find its central meaning.

IV. KINDS OF QUESTIONS

1. Multiple-choice Questions

Most popular of the short-answer questions is the "multiple choice" or "best answer" question. It can be used, for example, to test for factual knowledge, ability to solve problems or judgment in meeting situations found at work.

A multiple-choice question is normally one of three types:
- It can begin with an incomplete statement followed by several possible endings. You are to find the one ending which best completes the statement, although some of the others may not be entirely wrong.
- It can also be a complete statement in the form of a question which is answered by choosing one of the statements listed.
- It can be in the form of a problem – again you select the best answer.

Here is an example of a multiple-choice question with a discussion which should give you some clues as to the method for choosing the right answer:

When an employee has a complaint about his assignment, the action which will best help him overcome his difficulty is to
- A. discuss his difficulty with his coworkers
- B. take the problem to the head of the organization
- C. take the problem to the person who gave him the assignment
- D. say nothing to anyone about his complaint

In answering this question, you should study each of the choices to find which is best. Consider choice "A" – Certainly an employee may discuss his complaint with fellow employees, but no change or improvement can result, and the complaint remains unresolved. Choice "B" is a poor choice since the head of the organization probably does not know what assignment you have been given, and taking your problem to him is known as "going over the head" of the supervisor. The supervisor, or person who made the assignment, is the person who can clarify it or correct any injustice. Choice "C" is, therefore, correct. To say nothing, as in choice "D," is unwise. Supervisors have and interest in knowing the problems employees are facing, and the employee is seeking a solution to his problem.

2. True/False

3. Matching Questions

Matching an answer from a column of choices within another column.

V. RECORDING YOUR ANSWERS

Computer terminals are used more and more today for many different kinds of exams.

For an examination with very few applicants, you may be told to record your answers in the test booklet itself. Separate answer sheets are much more common. If this separate answer sheet is to be scored by machine – and this is often the case – it is highly important that you mark your answers correctly in order to get credit.

VI. BEFORE THE TEST

YOUR PHYSICAL CONDITION IS IMPORTANT

If you are not well, you can't do your best work on tests. If you are half asleep, you can't do your best either. Here are some tips:

1) Get about the same amount of sleep you usually get. Don't stay up all night before the test, either partying or worrying—DON'T DO IT!
2) If you wear glasses, be sure to wear them when you go to take the test. This goes for hearing aids, too.
3) If you have any physical problems that may keep you from doing your best, be sure to tell the person giving the test. If you are sick or in poor health, you relay cannot do your best on any test. You can always come back and take the test some other time.

Common sense will help you find procedures to follow to get ready for an examination. Too many of us, however, overlook these sensible measures. Indeed, nervousness and fatigue have been found to be the most serious reasons why applicants fail to do their best on civil service tests. Here is a list of reminders:

- Begin your preparation early – Don't wait until the last minute to go scurrying around for books and materials or to find out what the position is all about.
- Prepare continuously – An hour a night for a week is better than an all-night cram session. This has been definitely established. What is more, a night a week for a month will return better dividends than crowding your study into a shorter period of time.
- Locate the place of the exam – You have been sent a notice telling you when and where to report for the examination. If the location is in a different town or otherwise unfamiliar to you, it would be well to inquire the best route and learn something about the building.
- Relax the night before the test – Allow your mind to rest. Do not study at all that night. Plan some mild recreation or diversion; then go to bed early and get a good night's sleep.
- Get up early enough to make a leisurely trip to the place for the test – This way unforeseen events, traffic snarls, unfamiliar buildings, etc. will not upset you.
- Dress comfortably – A written test is not a fashion show. You will be known by number and not by name, so wear something comfortable.
- Leave excess paraphernalia at home – Shopping bags and odd bundles will get in your way. You need bring only the items mentioned in the official notice you received; usually everything you need is provided. Do not bring reference books to the exam. They will only confuse those last minutes and be taken away from you when in the test room.

- Arrive somewhat ahead of time – If because of transportation schedules you must get there very early, bring a newspaper or magazine to take your mind off yourself while waiting.
- Locate the examination room – When you have found the proper room, you will be directed to the seat or part of the room where you will sit. Sometimes you are given a sheet of instructions to read while you are waiting. Do not fill out any forms until you are told to do so; just read them and be prepared.
- Relax and prepare to listen to the instructions
- If you have any physical problem that may keep you from doing your best, be sure to tell the test administrator. If you are sick or in poor health, you really cannot do your best on the exam. You can come back and take the test some other time.

VII. AT THE TEST

The day of the test is here and you have the test booklet in your hand. The temptation to get going is very strong. Caution! There is more to success than knowing the right answers. You must know how to identify your papers and understand variations in the type of short-answer question used in this particular examination. Follow these suggestions for maximum results from your efforts:

1) Cooperate with the monitor

The test administrator has a duty to create a situation in which you can be as much at ease as possible. He will give instructions, tell you when to begin, check to see that you are marking your answer sheet correctly, and so on. He is not there to guard you, although he will see that your competitors do not take unfair advantage. He wants to help you do your best.

2) Listen to all instructions

Don't jump the gun! Wait until you understand all directions. In most civil service tests you get more time than you need to answer the questions. So don't be in a hurry. Read each word of instructions until you clearly understand the meaning. Study the examples, listen to all announcements and follow directions. Ask questions if you do not understand what to do.

3) Identify your papers

Civil service exams are usually identified by number only. You will be assigned a number; you must not put your name on your test papers. Be sure to copy your number correctly. Since more than one exam may be given, copy your exact examination title.

4) Plan your time

Unless you are told that a test is a "speed" or "rate of work" test, speed itself is usually not important. Time enough to answer all the questions will be provided, but this does not mean that you have all day. An overall time limit has been set. Divide the total time (in minutes) by the number of questions to determine the approximate time you have for each question.

5) Do not linger over difficult questions

If you come across a difficult question, mark it with a paper clip (useful to have along) and come back to it when you have been through the booklet. One caution if you do this – be sure to skip a number on your answer sheet as well. Check often to be sure that you have not lost your place and that you are marking in the row numbered the same as the question you are answering.

6) Read the questions

Be sure you know what the question asks! Many capable people are unsuccessful because they failed to read the questions correctly.

7) Answer all questions

Unless you have been instructed that a penalty will be deducted for incorrect answers, it is better to guess than to omit a question.

8) Speed tests

It is often better NOT to guess on speed tests. It has been found that on timed tests people are tempted to spend the last few seconds before time is called in marking answers at random – without even reading them – in the hope of picking up a few extra points. To discourage this practice, the instructions may warn you that your score will be "corrected" for guessing. That is, a penalty will be applied. The incorrect answers will be deducted from the correct ones, or some other penalty formula will be used.

9) Review your answers

If you finish before time is called, go back to the questions you guessed or omitted to give them further thought. Review other answers if you have time.

10) Return your test materials

If you are ready to leave before others have finished or time is called, take ALL your materials to the monitor and leave quietly. Never take any test material with you. The monitor can discover whose papers are not complete, and taking a test booklet may be grounds for disqualification.

VIII. EXAMINATION TECHNIQUES

1) Read the general instructions carefully. These are usually printed on the first page of the exam booklet. As a rule, these instructions refer to the timing of the examination; the fact that you should not start work until the signal and must stop work at a signal, etc. If there are any special instructions, such as a choice of questions to be answered, make sure that you note this instruction carefully.

2) When you are ready to start work on the examination, that is as soon as the signal has been given, read the instructions to each question booklet, underline any key words or phrases, such as least, best, outline, describe and the like. In this way you will tend to answer as requested rather than discover on reviewing your paper that you listed without describing, that you selected the worst choice rather than the best choice, etc.

3) If the examination is of the objective or multiple-choice type – that is, each question will also give a series of possible answers: A, B, C or D, and you are called upon to select the best answer and write the letter next to that answer on your answer paper – it is advisable to start answering each question in turn. There may be anywhere from 50 to 100 such questions in the three or four hours allotted and you can see how much time would be taken if you read through all the questions before beginning to answer any. Furthermore, if you

come across a question or group of questions which you know would be difficult to answer, it would undoubtedly affect your handling of all the other questions.

4) If the examination is of the essay type and contains but a few questions, it is a moot point as to whether you should read all the questions before starting to answer any one. Of course, if you are given a choice – say five out of seven and the like – then it is essential to read all the questions so you can eliminate the two that are most difficult. If, however, you are asked to answer all the questions, there may be danger in trying to answer the easiest one first because you may find that you will spend too much time on it. The best technique is to answer the first question, then proceed to the second, etc.

5) Time your answers. Before the exam begins, write down the time it started, then add the time allowed for the examination and write down the time it must be completed, then divide the time available somewhat as follows:
   - If 3-1/2 hours are allowed, that would be 210 minutes. If you have 80 objective-type questions, that would be an average of 2-1/2 minutes per question. Allow yourself no more than 2 minutes per question, or a total of 160 minutes, which will permit about 50 minutes to review.
   - If for the time allotment of 210 minutes there are 7 essay questions to answer, that would average about 30 minutes a question. Give yourself only 25 minutes per question so that you have about 35 minutes to review.

6) The most important instruction is to read each question and make sure you know what is wanted. The second most important instruction is to time yourself properly so that you answer every question. The third most important instruction is to answer every question. Guess if you have to but include something for each question. Remember that you will receive no credit for a blank and will probably receive some credit if you write something in answer to an essay question. If you guess a letter – say "B" for a multiple-choice question – you may have guessed right. If you leave a blank as an answer to a multiple-choice question, the examiners may respect your feelings but it will not add a point to your score. Some exams may penalize you for wrong answers, so in such cases only, you may not want to guess unless you have some basis for your answer.

7) Suggestions
   a. Objective-type questions
      1. Examine the question booklet for proper sequence of pages and questions
      2. Read all instructions carefully
      3. Skip any question which seems too difficult; return to it after all other questions have been answered
      4. Apportion your time properly; do not spend too much time on any single question or group of questions
      5. Note and underline key words – all, most, fewest, least, best, worst, same, opposite, etc.
      6. Pay particular attention to negatives
      7. Note unusual option, e.g., unduly long, short, complex, different or similar in content to the body of the question
      8. Observe the use of "hedging" words – probably, may, most likely, etc.

9. Make sure that your answer is put next to the same number as the question
10. Do not second-guess unless you have good reason to believe the second answer is definitely more correct
11. Cross out original answer if you decide another answer is more accurate; do not erase until you are ready to hand your paper in
12. Answer all questions; guess unless instructed otherwise
13. Leave time for review

b. Essay questions
1. Read each question carefully
2. Determine exactly what is wanted. Underline key words or phrases.
3. Decide on outline or paragraph answer
4. Include many different points and elements unless asked to develop any one or two points or elements
5. Show impartiality by giving pros and cons unless directed to select one side only
6. Make and write down any assumptions you find necessary to answer the questions
7. Watch your English, grammar, punctuation and choice of words
8. Time your answers; don't crowd material

8) Answering the essay question

Most essay questions can be answered by framing the specific response around several key words or ideas. Here are a few such key words or ideas:

M's: manpower, materials, methods, money, management
P's: purpose, program, policy, plan, procedure, practice, problems, pitfalls, personnel, public relations

a. Six basic steps in handling problems:
1. Preliminary plan and background development
2. Collect information, data and facts
3. Analyze and interpret information, data and facts
4. Analyze and develop solutions as well as make recommendations
5. Prepare report and sell recommendations
6. Install recommendations and follow up effectiveness

b. Pitfalls to avoid
1. Taking things for granted – A statement of the situation does not necessarily imply that each of the elements is necessarily true; for example, a complaint may be invalid and biased so that all that can be taken for granted is that a complaint has been registered
2. Considering only one side of a situation – Wherever possible, indicate several alternatives and then point out the reasons you selected the best one
3. Failing to indicate follow up – Whenever your answer indicates action on your part, make certain that you will take proper follow-up action to see how successful your recommendations, procedures or actions turn out to be
4. Taking too long in answering any single question – Remember to time your answers properly

EXAMINATION SECTION

PREPARING WRITTEN MATERIAL

I. COMMENTARY

The need to communicate-- clearly, swiftly, completely, effectively -- is basic to all organizations, agencies, departments --public and private, large and small.

Communication is accomplished by employing one or more of the accepted forms of communication, singly and/or together -- oral (verbal), written, visual, electronic, etc.

The method most often used to reach large numbers or groups of persons to achieve and ensure clarity, correctness, comprehension, uniformity, and permanence of effect, is through the preparation and issuance of written materials, e.g., notices, statements, letters, reports, descriptions, explanations, expositions, schedules, summaries, etc.

Preparing written material clearly and correctly is, therefore, a dutiable function of every regular and senior employee, foreman, supervisor, manager, administrator, director; and this quest ion-type is often used as a basic, integral part of various selection processes.

Questions involving correctness of expression usually appear on career written examinations as well as on other types of general tests.

While this question-type may take several forms, the two most usual presentations are the single-sentence type, which is to be evaluated as correct or incorrect on one of several bases, and the multiple-sentence type, involving four or five sentences, one of which is to be denoted as correct (or incorrect) for reasons of grammar and usage, or correctness of expression.

DIRECTIONS AND SAMPLE QUESTIONS

DIRECTIONS

Each of the sentences numbered I and II may be classified under one of the following four categories:

- A. *Faulty* because of incorrect grammar or word usage
- B. *Faulty* because of incorrect punctuation
- C. *Faulty* because of incorrect capitalization or incorrect spelling
- D. *Correct*

Examine each sentence carefully to determine under which of the above four options it is best classified. Then, in the space to the right, print the capital letter preceding the option which is the best of the four suggested above.

SAMPLE QUESTIONS

I. One of our clerks were promoted yesterday.   I.____

The subject of this sentence is "one," so the verb should be "was promoted" instead of "were promoted." Since the sentence is incorrect because of bad grammar, the answer to Sample Question I Is (A)

II. Between you and me, I would prefer not going there.   II.____

Since this sentence is correct, the answer to Sample Question II is (D)

PREPARING WRITTEN MATERIAL

II. COMMON ERRORS/CORRECT USES

Common Errors in Usage

1. being that for since
2. like for as
3. off of for-off
4. different than for different from
5. quick for quickly
6. careful for carefully
7. sure for surely
8. good for well
9. nothing for anything
10. most for almost
11. real for really
12. this here for this
13. swell for excellent
14. well for good
15. those for that (kind)
16. less for fewer
17. them for those
18. they for he
19. him for he (after than)
20. their for his
21. who for whom
22. whom for who
23. I for me
24. are for is
25. tore for torn
26. wrote for-written
27. busted for burst
28. seen for saw
29. done for did
30. graduated for graduated from
31. irregardless for regardless
32. am living for have been living
33. laying for lying
34. leave for let
35. should of for should have
36. except for accept
37. besides for beside
38. affect for effect

39. amount for number
40. kind of a for kind of

Correct Usage

1. Since he was late, he was not admitted.
2. She smiles as her father does.
3. He took his hat off his head
4. Your pen is different from mine
5. Go quickly
6. He laid the tray down carefully.
7. The boy was surely happy to hear this.
8. I cannot hear well.
9. I didn't see anything.
10. Almost everyone was there.
11. The baby is really beautiful.
12. This ball is broken.
13. That was an excellent play.
14. She looks good in her new suit.
15. I prefer that kind of cigarettes.
16. We have fewer bad marks than they.
17. Please take those knives away.
18. People can be what they want to be.
19. I am younger than he.
20. Every soldier will do his duty.
21. Whom do you think I met today?
22. Who do you think it was?
23. Between you and me ...
24. Everybody is here
25. He had torn the manuscript in two.
26. I have written a play.
27. The bubble burst.
28. I saw the new boy.
29. He did it.
30. He graduated from Lincoln High.
31. Regardless of the weather, we will fly.
32. I have been living here for a month.
33. He was lying on the ground.
34. Let him go.
35. I should have thought of that.
36. I accept your apology.
37. I shall sit beside you.
38. The motion picture HOLOCAUST had a great effect on all who saw it.

39. We have a large number of books in the library.
40. What kind of car do you have?

PREPARING WRITTEN MATERIAL
EXAMINATION SECTION
TEST 1

DIRECTIONS: Each of the sentences in this test may be classified under one of the following four categories:
- A. Faulty because of incorrect grammar or word usage
- B. Faulty because of incorrect punctuation
- C. Faulty because of incorrect capitalization or incorrect spelling
- D. Correct

Examine each sentence carefully to determine under which of the above four options it is best classified. Then, in the space to the right, print the capital letter preceding the option which is the BEST of the four suggested above. (Note that each faulty sentence contains but one type of error. Consider a sentence to be correct if it contains none of the types of errors mentioned, even though there may be other correct ways of expressing the same thought.)

1. He sent the notice to the clerk who you hired yesterday. 1.____
2. It must be admitted, however that you were not informed of this change. 2.____
3. Only the employee who have served in this grade for at least two years are eligible for promotion. 3.____
4. The work was divided equally between she and Mary. 4.____
5. He thought that you were not available at that time. 5.____
6. When the messenger returns; please give him this package. 6.____
7. The new secretary prepared, typed, addressed, and delivered, the notices. 7.____
8. Walking into the room, his desk can be seen at the rear. 8.____
9. Although John has worked here longer than She, he produces a smaller amount of work. 9.____
10. She said she could of typed this report yesterday. 10.____
11. Neither one of these procedures are adequate for the efficient performance of this task. 11.____
12. The typewriter is the tool of the typist; the cash register, the tool of the cashier. 12.____

13. "The assignment must be completed as soon as possible" said the supervisor. 13.____

14. As you know, office handbooks are issued to all new Employees. 14.____

15. Writing a speech is sometimes easier than to deliver it before an audience. 15.____

16. Mr. Brown our accountant, will audit the accounts next week. 16.____

17. Give the assignment to whomever is able to do it most efficiently. 17.____

18. The supervisor expected either your or I to file these reports. 18.____

KEY (CORRECT ANSWERS)

1.	A	11.	A
2.	B	12.	C
3.	D	13.	B
4.	A	14.	C
5.	D	15.	A
6.	B	16.	B
7.	B	17.	A
8.	A	18.	A
9.	C		
10.	A		

TEST 2

DIRECTIONS: Each of the sentences in this test may be classified under one of the following four categories:
- A. Faulty because of incorrect grammar or word usage
- B. Faulty because of incorrect punctuation
- C. Faulty because of incorrect capitalization or incorrect spelling
- D. Correct

Examine each sentence carefully to determine under which of the above four options it is best classified. Then, in the space to the right, print the capital letter preceding the option which is the BEST of the four suggested above. (Note that each faulty sentence contains but one type of error. Consider a sentence to be correct if it contains none of the types of errors mentioned, even though there may be other correct ways of expressing the same thought.)

1. The fire apparently started in the storeroom, which is usually locked. 1.____
2. On approaching the victim, two bruises were noticed by this officer. 2.____
3. The officer, who was there examined the report with great care. 3.____
4. Each employee in the office had a seperate desk. 4.____
5. All employees including members of the clerical staff, were invited to the lecture. 5.____
6. The suggested Procedure is similar to the one now in use. 6.____
7. No one was more pleased with the new procedure than the chauffeur. 7.____
8. He tried to persaude her to change the procedure. 8.____
9. The total of the expenses charged to petty cash were high. 9.____
10. An understanding between him and I was finally reached. 10.____

KEY (CORRECT ANSWERS)

1.	D	6.	C
2.	A	7.	D
3.	B	8.	C
4.	C	9.	A
5.	B	10.	A

TEST 3

DIRECTIONS: Each of the sentences in this test may be classified under one of the following four categories:
- A. Faulty because of incorrect grammar or word usage
- B. Faulty because of incorrect punctuation
- C. Faulty because of incorrect capitalization or incorrect spelling
- D. Correct

Examine each sentence carefully to determine under which of the above four options it is best classified. Then, in the space to the right, print the capital letter preceding the option which is the BEST of the four suggested above. (Note that each faulty sentence contains but one type of error. Consider a sentence to be correct if it contains none of the types of errors mentioned, even though there may be other correct ways of expressing the same thought.)

1. They told both he and I that the prisoner had escaped. 1.____

2. Any superior officer, who, disregards the just complaint of his subordinates, is remiss in the performance of his duty. 2.____

3. Only those members of the national organization who resided in the Middle West attended the conference in Chicago. 3.____

4. We told him to give the national organization assignment to whoever was available. 4.____

5. Please do not disappoint and embarass us by not appearing in court. 5.____

6. Although the office's speech proved to be entertaining, the topic was not relevent to the main theme of the conference. 6.____

7. In February all new officers attended a training course in which they were learned in their principal duties and the fundamental operating procedure of the department. 7.____

8. I personally seen inmate Jones threaten inmates Smith and Green with bodily harm if they refused to participate in the plot. 8.____

9. To the layman, who on a chance visit to the prison observes everything functioning smoothly, the maintenance of prison discipline may seem to be a relatively easily realizable objective. 9.____

10. The prisoners in cell block fourty were forbidden to sit on the cell cots during the recreation hour. 10.____

KEY (CORRECT ANSWERS)

1.	A	6.	C
2.	B	7.	A
3.	C	8.	A
4.	D	9.	D
5.	C	10.	C

TEST 4

DIRECTIONS: Each of the sentences in this test may be classified under one of the following four categories:
- A. Faulty because of incorrect grammar or word usage
- B. Faulty because of incorrect punctuation
- C. Faulty because of incorrect capitalization or incorrect spelling
- D. Correct

Examine each sentence carefully to determine under which of the above four options it is best classified. Then, in the space to the right, print the capital letter preceding the option which is the BEST of the four suggested above. (Note that each faulty sentence contains but one type of error. Consider a sentence to be correct if it contains none of the types of errors mentioned, even though there may be other correct ways of expressing the same thought.)

1. I cannot encourage you any.   1.____
2. You always look well in those sort of clothes.   2.____
3. Shall we go to the park?   3.____
4. The man whome he introduced was Mr. Carey.   4.____
5. She saw the letter laying here this morning.   5.____
6. It should rain before the Afternoon is over.   6.____
7. They have already went home.   7.____
8. That Jackson will be elected is evident.   8.____
9. He does not hardly approve of us.   9.____
10. It was he, who won the prize.   10.____

KEY (CORRECT ANSWERS)

1.	A	6.	C
2.	A	7.	A
3.	D	8.	D
4.	C	9.	A
5.	A	10.	B

TEST 5

DIRECTIONS: Each of the sentences in this test may be classified under one of the following four categories:
    A. Faulty because of incorrect grammar or word usage
    B. Faulty because of incorrect punctuation
    C. Faulty because of incorrect capitalization or incorrect spelling
    D. Correct

Examine each sentence carefully to determine under which of the above four options it is best classified. Then, in the space to the right, print the capital letter preceding the option which is the BEST of the four suggested above. (Note that each faulty sentence contains but one type of error. Consider a sentence to be correct if it contains none of the types of errors mentioned, even though there may be other correct ways of expressing the same thought.)

1. Shall we go to the park.
2. They are, alike, in this particular way.
3. They gave the poor man sume food when he knocked on the door.
4. I regret the loss caused by the error.
5. The students' will have a new teacher.
6. They sweared to bring out all the facts.
7. He decided to open a branch store on 33rd street.
8. His speed is equal and more than that of a racehorse.
9. He felt very warm on that Summer day.
10. He was assisted by his friend, who lives in the next house.

KEY (CORRECT ANSWERS)

1. B
2. B
3. C
4. D
5. B
6. A
7. C
8. A
9. C
10. D

TEST 6

DIRECTIONS: Each of the sentences in this test may be classified under one of the following four categories:
- A. Faulty because of incorrect grammar or word usage
- B. Faulty because of incorrect punctuation
- C. Faulty because of incorrect capitalization or incorrect spelling
- D. Correct

Examine each sentence carefully to determine under which of the above four options it is best classified. Then, in the space to the right, print the capital letter preceding the option which is the BEST of the four suggested above. (Note that each faulty sentence contains but one type of error. Consider a sentence to be correct if it contains none of the types of errors mentioned, even though there may be other correct ways of expressing the same thought.)

1. The climate of New York is colder than California. 1.____
2. I shall wait for you on the corner. 2.____
3. Did we see the boy who, we think, is the leader. 3.____
4. Being a modest person, John seldom talks about his invention. 4.____
5. The gang is called the smith street bos. 5.____
6. He seen the man break into the store. 6.____
7. We expected to lay still there for quite a while. 7.____
8. He is considered to be the Leader of his organization. 8.____
9. Although I recieved an invitation, I won't go. 9.____
10. The letter must be here some place. 10.____

KEY (CORRECT ANSWERS)

1. A   6. A
2. D   7. A
3. B   8. C
4. D   9. C
5. C   10. A

TEST 7

DIRECTIONS: Each of the sentences in this test may be classified under one of the following four categories:
- A. Faulty because of incorrect grammar or word usage
- B. Faulty because of incorrect punctuation
- C. Faulty because of incorrect capitalization or incorrect spelling
- D. Correct

Examine each sentence carefully to determine under which of the above four options it is best classified. Then, in the space to the right, print the capital letter preceding the option which is the BEST of the four suggested above. (Note that each faulty sentence contains but one type of error. Consider a sentence to be correct if it contains none of the types of errors mentioned, even though there may be other correct ways of expressing the same thought.)

1. I though it to be he.   1.____
2. We expect to remain here for a long time.   2.____
3. The committee was agreed.   3.____
4. Two-thirds of the building are finished.   4.____
5. The water was froze.   5.____
6. Everyone of the salesmen must supply their own car.   6.____
7. Who is the author of Gone With the Wind?   7.____
8. He marched on and declaring that he would never surrender.   8.____
9. Who shall I say called?   9.____
10. Everyone has left but they.   10.____

KEY (CORRECT ANSWERS)

1.	A	6.	A
2.	D	7.	B
3.	D	8.	A
4.	A	9.	D
5.	A	10.	D

TEST 8

DIRECTIONS: Each of the sentences in this test may be classified under one of the following four categories:
- A. Faulty because of incorrect grammar or word usage
- B. Faulty because of incorrect punctuation
- C. Faulty because of incorrect capitalization or incorrect spelling
- D. Correct

Examine each sentence carefully to determine under which of the above four options it is best classified. Then, in the space to the right, print the capital letter preceding the option which is the BEST of the four suggested above. (Note that each faulty sentence contains but one type of error. Consider a sentence to be correct if it contains none of the types of errors mentioned, even though there may be other correct ways of expressing the same thought.)

1. Who did we give the order to?   1.____
2. Send your order in immediately.   2.____
3. I believe I paid the Bill.   3.____
4. I have not met but one person.   4.____
5. Why aren't Tom, and Fred, going to the dance?   5.____
6. What reason is there for him not going?   6.____
7. The seige of Malta was a tremendous event.   7.____
8. I was there yesterday I assure you   8.____
9. Your ukulele is better than mine.   9.____
10. No one was there only Mary.   10.____

KEY (CORRECT ANSWERS)

1.	A	6.	A
2.	D	7.	C
3.	C	8.	B
4.	A	9.	C
5.	B	10.	A

TEST 9

DIRECTIONS: In each of the following groups of sentences, one of the four sentences is faulty in grammar, punctuation, or capitalization. Select the INCORRECT sentence in each case.

1. A. If you had stood at home and done your homework, you would not have failed in arithmetic.
   B. Her affected manner annoyed every member of the audience.
   C. How will the new law affect our income taxes?
   D. The plants were not affected by the long, cold winter, but they succumbed to the drought of summer.

   1.____

2. A. He is one of the most able men who have been in the Senate.
   B. It is he who is to blame for the lamentable mistake.
   C. Haven't you a helpful suggestion to make at this time?
   D. The money was robbed from the blind man's cup.

   2.____

3. A. The amount of children in this school is steadily increasing.
   B. After taking an apple from the table, she went out to play.
   C. He borrowed a dollar from me.
   D. I had hoped my brother would arrive before me.

   3.____

4. A. Whom do you think I hear from every week?
   B. Who do you think is the right man for the job?
   C. Who do you think I found in the room?
   D. He is the man whom we considered a good candidate for the presidency.

   4.____

5. A. Quietly the puppy laid down before the fireplace.
   B. You have made your bed; now lie in it.
   C. I was badly sunburned because I had lain too long in the sun.
   D. I laid the doll on the bed and left the room.

   5.____

KEY (CORRECT ANSWERS)

1. A
2. D
3. A
4. C
5. A

PREPARING WRITTEN MATERIAL
EXAMINATION SECTION
TEST 1

DIRECTIONS: Each of the sentences in this test may be classified under one of the following four categories:
- A. *Incorrect* because of faulty grammar or sentence structure
- B. *Incorrect* because of faulty punctuation
- C. *Incorrect* because of faulty capitalization
- D. *Correct*

Examine each sentence carefully to determine under which of the above four options it is best classified. Then, in the space at the right, print the capital letter preceding the option which is the BEST of the four suggested above.

(Each incorrect sentence contains but one type of error. Consider a sentence to be correct if it contains none of the types of errors mentioned, even though there may be other correct ways of expressing the same thought.)

1. This fact, together with those brought out at the previous meeting, prove that the schedule is satisfactory to the employees.   1.____

2. Like many employees in scientific fields, the work of bookkeepers and accountants requires accuracy and neatness.   2.____

3. "What can I do for you," the secretary asked as she motioned to the visitor to take a seat.   3.____

4. Our representative, Mr. Charles will call on you next week to determine whether or not your claim has merit.   4.____

5. We expect you to return in the spring; please do not disappoint us.   5.____

6. Any supervisor, who disregards the just complaints of his subordinates, is remiss in the performance of his duty.   6.____

7. Because she took less than an hour for lunch is no reason for permitting her to leave before five o'clock.   7.____

8. "Miss Smith," said the supervisor, "Please arrange a meeting of the staff for two o'clock on Monday."   8.____

9. A private company's vacation and sick leave allowance usually differs considerably from a public agency.   9.____

10. Therefore, in order to increase the efficiency of operations in the department, a report on the recommended changes in procedures was presented to the departmental committee in charge of the program.   10.____

11. We told him to assign the work to whoever was available. 11._____

12. Since John was the most efficient of any other employee in the bureau, he received the highest service rating. 12._____

13. Only those members of the national organization who resided in the middle West attended the conference in Chicago. 13._____

14. The question of whether the office manager has as yet attained, or indeed can ever hope to secure professional status is one which has been discussed for years. 14._____

15. No one knew who to blame for the error which, we later discovered, resulted in a considerable loss of time. 15._____

KEY (CORRECT ANSWERS)

1.	A	6.	B	11.	D
2.	A	7.	A	12.	A
3.	B	8.	C	13.	C
4.	B	9.	A	14.	B
5.	D	10.	D	15.	A

TEST 2

DIRECTIONS: Each of the sentences in this test may be classified under one of the following four categories:
- A. *Incorrect* because of faulty grammar or sentence structure
- B. *Incorrect* because of faulty punctuation
- C. *Incorrect* because of faulty capitalization
- D. *Correct*

1. The National alliance of Businessmen is trying to persuade private businesses to hire youth in the summertime. 1._____

2. The supervisor who is on vacation, is in charge of processing vouchers. 2._____

3. The activity of the committee at its conferences is always stimulating. 3._____

4. After checking the addresses again, the letters went to the mailroom. 4._____

5. The director, as well as the employees, are interested in sharing the dividends. 5._____

KEY (CORRECT ANSWERS)

1. C
2. B
3. D
4. A
5. A

TEST 3

DIRECTIONS: In each of the following groups of sentences, one of the four sentences is faulty in grammar, punctuation, or capitalization. Select the INCORRECT sentence in each case.

1. A. Sailing down the bay was a thrilling experience for me.
   B. He was not consulted about your joining the club.
   C. This story is different than the one I told you yesterday.
   D. There is no doubt about his being the best player.

   1.____

2. A. He maintains there is but one road to world peace.
   B. It is common knowledge that a child sees much he is not supposed to see.
   C. Much of the bitterness might have been avoided if arbitration had been resorted to earlier in the meeting.
   D. The man decided it would be advisable to marry a girl somewhat younger than him.

   2.____

3. A. In this book, the incident I liked least is where the hero tries to put out the forest fire.
   B. Learning a foreign language will undoubtedly give a person a better understanding of his mother tongue.
   C. His actions made us wonder what he planned to do next.
   D. Because of the war, we were unable to travel during the summer vacation.

   3.____

4. A. The class had no sooner become interested in the lesson than the dismissal bell rang.
   B. There is little agreement about the kind of world to be planned at the peace conference.
   C. "Today," said the teacher, "we shall read 'The Wind in the Willows,' I am sure you'll like it.
   D. The terms of the legal settlement of the family quarrel handicapped both sides for many years.

   4.____

5. A. I was so surprised that I was not able to say a word.
   B. She is taller than any other member of the class.
   C. It would be much more preferable if you were never seen in his company.
   D. We had no choice but to excuse her for being late.

   5.____

KEY (CORRECT ANSWERS)

1. C
2. D
3. A
4. C
5. C

TEST 4

DIRECTIONS: In each of the following groups of sentences, one of the four sentences is faulty in grammar, punctuation, or capitalization. Select the INCORRECT sentence in each case.

1.
   A. Please send me these data at the earliest opportunity.
   B. The loss of their material proved to be a severe handicap.
   C. My principal objection to this plan is that it is impracticable.
   D. The doll had laid in the rain for an hour and was ruined.

   1.____

2.
   A. The garden scissors, left out all night in the rain, were in a badly rusted condition.
   B. The girls felt bad about the misunderstanding which had arisen
   C. Sitting near the campfire, the old man told John and I about many exciting adventures he had had.
   D. Neither of us is in a position to undertake a task of that magnitude.

   2.____

3.
   A. The general concluded that one of the three roads would lead to the besieged city.
   B. The children didn't, as a rule, do hardly anything beyond what they were told to do.
   C. The reason the girl gave for her negligence was that she had acted on the spur of the moment.
   D. The daffodils and tulips look beautiful in that blue vase.

   3.____

4.
   A. If I was ten years older, I should be interested in this work.
   B. Give the prize to whoever has drawn the best picture.
   C. When you have finished reading the book, take it back to the library.
   D. My drawing is as good as or better than yours.

   4.____

5.
   A. He asked me whether the substance was animal or vegetable.
   B. An apple which is unripe should not be eaten by a child.
   C. That was an insult to me who am your friend.
   D. Some spy must of reported the matter to the enemy.

   5.____

6.
   A. Limited time makes quoting the entire message impossible.
   B. Who did she say was going?
   C. The girls in your class have dressed more dolls this year than we.
   D. There was such a large amount of books on the floor that I couldn't find a place for my rocking chair.

   6.____

7.
   A. What with his sleeplessness and his ill health, he was unable to assume any responsibility for the success of the meeting.
   B. If I had been born in February, I should be celebrating my birthday soon.
   C. In order to prevent breakage, she placed a sheet of paper between each of the plates when she packed them.
   D. After the spring shower, the violets smelled very sweet.

   7.____

2 (#4)

8. A. He had laid the book down very reluctantly before the end of the lesson.   8.____
    B. The dog, I am sorry to say, had lain on the bed all night.
    C. The cloth was first lain on a flat surface; then it was pressed with a hot iron.
    D. While we were in Florida, we lay in the sun until we were noticeably tanned.

9. A. If John was in New York during the recent holiday season, I have no doubt   9.____
       he spent most of the time with his parents.
    B. How could he enjoy the television program; the dog was barking and the
       baby was crying.
    C. When the problem was explained to the class, he must have been asleep.
    D. She wished that her new dress were finished so that she could go to the
       party.

10. A. The engine not only furnishes power but light and heat as well.   10.____
    B. You're aware that we've forgotten whose guilt was established, aren't you?
    C. Everybody knows that the woman made many sacrifices for her children.
    D. A man with his dog and gun is a familiar sight in this neighborhood.

KEY (CORRECT ANSWERS)

1. D   6. D
2. C   7. B
3. B   8. C
4. A   9. B
5. D   10. A

TEST 5

DIRECTIONS: Each of Questions 1 through 5 consists of a sentence which may be classified appropriately under one of the following four categories:
A. *Incorrect* because of faulty grammar
B. *Incorrect* because of faulty punctuation
C. *Incorrect* because of faulty spelling
D. *Correct*

Examine each sentence carefully. Then, print in the space at the right the letter preceding the category which is the BEST of the four suggested above
(Note: Each incorrect sentence contains only one type of error. Consider a sentence correct if it contains no errors, although there may be other correct ways of writing the sentence.)

1. Of the two employees, the one in our office is the most efficient.   1._____

2. No one can apply or even understand, the new rules and regulations.   2._____

3. A large amount of supplies were stored in the empty office.   3._____

4. If an employee is occassionally asked to work overtime, he should do so willingly.   4._____

5. It is true that the new procedures are difficult to use but, we are certain that you will learn them quickly.   5._____

6. The office manager said that he did not know who would be given a large allotment under the new plan.   6._____

7. It was at the supervisor's request that the clerk agreed to postpone his vacation.   7._____

8. We do not believe that it is necessary for both he and the clerk to attend the conference.   8._____

9. All employees, who display perseverance, will be given adequate recognition.   9._____

10. He regrets that some of us employees are dissatisfied with our new assignments.   10._____

11. "Do you think that the raise was merited," asked the supervisor?   11._____

12. The new manual of procedure is a valuable supplament to our rules and regulations.   12._____

13. The typist admitted that she had attempted to pursuade the other employees to assist her in her work.   13._____

14. The supervisor asked that all amendments to the regulations be handled by you and I.   14.____

15. The custodian seen the boy who broke the window.   15.____

KEY (CORRECT ANSWERS)

1.	A	6.	D	11.	B
2.	B	7.	D	12.	C
3.	A	8.	A	13.	C
4.	C	9.	B	14.	A
5.	B	10.	D	15.	A

PREPARING WRITTEN MATERIAL
EXAMINATION SECTION
TEST 1

DIRECTIONS: The sentences numbered 1 to 10 deal with some phase of police activity. They may be classified most appropriately under one of the following four categories:
A. *Faulty* because of incorrect grammar
B. *Faulty* because of incorrect punctuation
C. *Faulty* because of incorrect use of a word
D. *Correct*

Examine each sentence carefully. Then, in the correspondingly numbered space on the right, print the capital letter preceding the option which is the best of the four suggested above.

(All incorrect sentences contain only one type of error. Consider a sentence correct if it contains none of the types of errors mentioned, even though there may be other correct ways of expressing the same thought.)

1. The Department Medal of Honor is awarded to a member of the Police Force who distinguishes himself inconspicuously in the line of police duty by the performance of an act of gallantry.   1.____

2. Members of the Detective Division are charged with: the prevention of crime, the detection and arrest of criminals, and the recovery of lost or stolen property.   2.____

3. Detectives are selected from the uniformed patrol forces after they have indicated by conduct, aptitude, and performance that they are qualified for the more intricate duties of a detective.   3.____

4. The patrolman, pursuing his assailant, exchanged shots with the gunman and immortally wounded him as he fled into a nearby building.   4.____

5. The members of the Traffic Division has to enforce the Vehicle and Traffic Law, the Traffic Regulations, and ordinances relating to vehicular and pedestrian traffic.   5.____

6. After firing a shot at the gunman, the crowd dispersed from the patrolman's line of fire.   6.____

7. The efficiency of the Missing Persons Bureau is maintained with a maximum of public personnel due to the specialized training given to its members.   7.____

8. Records of persons arrested for violations of Vehicle and Traffic Regulations are transmitted upon request to precincts, courts, and other authorized agencies.   8.____

2 (#1)

9. The arresting officer done all he could to subdue the perpetrator without physically injuring him. 9._____

10. The Deputy Commissioner is authorized to exercise all of the powers and duties of the Police Commissioner in the latter's absence. 10._____

KEY (CORRECT ANSWERS)

1. C 6. A
2. B 7. C
3. D 8. D
4. C 9. A
5. A 10. D

TEST 2

DIRECTIONS: Questions 1 through 4 consist of sentences concerning criminal law. Some of the sentences contain errors in English grammar or usage, punctuation, spelling, or capitalization. (A sentence does not contain an error simply because it could be written in a different manner.

Choose answer
A. if the sentence contains an error in English grammar or usage
B. if the sentence contains an error in punctuation
C. if the sentence contains an error in spelling or capitalization
D. if the sentence does not contain any errors

1. The severity of the sentence prescribed by contemporary statutes—including both the former and the revised New York Penal Laws—do not depend on what crime was intended by the offender.

2. It is generally recognized that two defects in the early law of *attempt* played a part in the birth of *burglary*: (1) immunity from prosecution for conduct short of the last act before completion of the crime, and (2) the relatively minor penalty imposed for an attempt (its being a common law misdemeanor) vis-à-a the completed offense.

3. The first sentence of the statute is applicable to employees who enter their place of employment, invited guests, and all other persons who have an express or implied license or privilege to enter the premises.

4. Contemporary criminal codes in the United States generally divide burglary into various degrees, differentiating the categories according to place, time, and other attendent circumstances.

KEY (CORRECT ANSWERS)

1. A
2. D
3. D
4. C

TEST 3

DIRECTIONS: For each of the sentences numbered 1 through 10, select from the options given below the MOST applicable choice, and print the letter of the correct answer in the space at the right.

    A. The sentence is correct.
    B. The sentence contains a spelling error only
    C. The sentence contains an English grammar error only
    D. The sentence contains *both* a spelling error and an English grammar error

1. Every person in the group is going to do his share.   1.____
2. The man who we selected is new to Duke University.   2.____
3. She is the older of the four secretaries on the two staffs that are to be combined.   3.____
4. The decision has to be made between him and I.   4.____
5. One of the volunteers are too young for this complecated task, don't you think?   5.____
6. I think your idea is splindid and it will improve this report considerably.   6.____
7. Do you think this is an exagerated account of the behavior you and me observed this morning?   7.____
8. Our supervisor has a clear idea of excelence.   8.____
9. How many occurences were verified by the observers?   9.____
10. We must complete the typing of the draft of the questionaire by noon tomorrow.   10.____

KEY (CORRECT ANSWERS)

1. A   6. B
2. C   7. D
3. C   8. B
4. C   9. B
5. D   10. B

TEST 4

DIRECTIONS: Questions 1 through 3 are based on the following paragraph, which consists of three numbered sentences.

Edit each sentence to insure clarity of meaning and correctness of grammar without substantially changing the meaning of the sentence.

Examine each sentence and then select the option which changes the sentence to express BEST the thought of the sentence.

(1) Unquestionably, a knowledge of business and finance is a good advantage to audit committee members but not essential to all members. (2) Other factors also carry weight; for example, at least one member must have the ability to preside over meetings and to discuss things along constructive lines. (3) In the same way, such factors as the amount of time a member can be able to devote to duties or his rating on the score of motivation, inquisitiveness, persistence, and disposition towards critical analysis are important.

1. In the first sentence, the word
   A. "good" should be changed to "distinct"
   B. "good" should be omitted
   C. "and" should be changed to "or"
   D. "are" should be inserted between the words "but" and "not"

2. In the second sentence, the
   A. word "factors" should be changed to "things"
   B. words "preside over" should be changed to "lead at"
   C. phrase "discuss things" should be changed to "direct the "discussion"
   D. word "constructive" should be changed to "noteworthy"

3. In the third sentence, the
   A. word "amount" should be changed to "period"
   B. words "amount of" should be changed to "length of"
   C. word "can" should be changed to "will"
   D. word "same" should be changed to "similar

KEY (CORRECT ANSWERS)

1. A
2. C
3. C

TEST 5

DIRECTIONS: Each question or incomplete statement is followed by several suggested answers or completions. Select the one that BEST answers the question or completes the statement. *PRINT THE LETTER OF THE CORRECT ANSWER IN THE SPACE AT THE RIGHT.*

1. Of the following, the MOST acceptable close of a business letter would usually be:
   A. Cordially yours,
   B. Respectfully Yours,
   C. Sincerely Yours,
   D. Yours very truly,

   1.____

2. When writing official correspondence to members of the armed forces, their titles should be used
   A. both on the envelope and in the inside address
   B. in the inside address, but not on the envelope
   C. neither on the envelope nor in the inside address
   D. on the envelope but not in the inside address

   2.____

3. Which one of the following is the LEAST important advantage of putting the subject of a letter in the heading to the right of the address? It
   A. makes filing of the copy easier
   B. makes more space available in the body of the letter
   C. simplifies distribution of letters
   D. simplifies determination of the subject of the letter

   3.____

4. Generally, when writing a letter, the use of precise words and concise sentences is
   A. *good*, because less time will be required to write the letter
   B. *bad*, because it is most likely that the reader will think the letter is unimportant and will not respond favorably
   C. *good*, because it is likely that your desired meaning will be conveyed to the reader
   D. *bad*, because your letter will be too brief to provide adequate information

   4.____

5. Of the following, it is MOST appropriate to use a form letter when it is necessary to answer many
   A. requests or inquiries from a single individual
   B. follow-up letters from individuals requesting additional information
   C. requests or inquiries about a single subject
   D. complaints from individuals that they have been unable to obtain various types of information

   5.____

KEY (CORRECT ANSWERS)

1. D
2. A
3. B
4. C
5. C

TEST 6

DIRECTIONS: Each question or incomplete statement is followed by several suggested answers or completions. Select the one that BEST answers the question or completes the statement. *PRINT THE LETTER OF THE CORRECT ANSWER IN THE SPACE AT THE RIGHT.*

1. The one of the following sentences which is LEAST acceptable from the viewpoint of correct usage is:
   A. The police thought the fugitive to be him.
   B. The criminals set a trap for whoever would fall into it.
   C. It is ten years ago since the fugitive fled from the city.
   D. The lecturer argued that criminals are usually cowards.
   E. The police removed four bucketfuls of earth from the scene of the crime.

   1._____

2. The one of the following sentences which is LEAST acceptable from the viewpoint of correct usage is:
   A. The patrolman scrutinized the report with great care.
   B. Approaching the victim of the assault, two bruises were noticed by the patrolman.
   C. As soon as I had broken down the door, I stepped into the room.
   D. I observed the accused loitering near the building, which was closed at the time.
   E. The storekeeper complained that his neighbor was guilty of violating a local ordinance.

   2._____

3. The one of the following sentences which is LEAST acceptable from the viewpoint of correct usage is:
   A. I realized immediately that he intended to assault the woman, so I disarmed him.
   B. It was apparent that Mr. Smith's explanation contained many inconsistencies.
   C. Despite the slippery condition of the street, he managed to stop the vehicle before injuring the child.
   D. Not a single one of them wish, despite the damage to property, to make a formal complaint.
   E. The body was found lying on the floor.

   3._____

KEY (CORRECT ANSWERS)

1. C
2. B
3. D

PREPARING WRITTEN MATERIAL
EXAMINATION SECTION
TEST 1

DIRECTIONS: Each of Questions 1 through 5 consists of a sentence which may or may not be an example of good formal English usage. Examine each sentence, considering grammar, punctuation, spelling, capitalization, and awkwardness. Then choose the correct statement about it from the four options below it. If the English usage in the sentence given is better than any of the changes suggested in options B, C, or D, pick option A. (Do not pick an option that will change the meaning of the sentence.) *PRINT THE LETTER OF THE CORRECT ANSWER IN THE SPACE AT THE RIGHT.*

1. I don't know who could possibly of broken it. 1.____
   A. This is an example of good formal English usage.
   B. The word "who" should be replaced by the word "whom."
   C. The word "of" should be replaced by the word "have."
   D. The word "broken" should be replaced by the word "broke."

2. Telephoning is easier than to write. 2.____
   A. This is an example of good formal English usage.
   B. The word "telephoning" should be spelled "telephoneing."
   C. The word "than" should be replaced by the word "then."
   D. The words "to write" should be replaced by the word "writing."

3. The two operators who have been assigned to these consoles are on vacation. 3.____
   A. This is an example of good formal English usage.
   B. A comma should be placed after the word "operators."
   C. The word "who" should be replaced by the word "whom."
   D. The word "are" should be replaced by the word "is."

4. You were suppose to teach me how to operate a plugboard. 4.____
   A. This is an example of good formal English usage.
   B. The word "were" should be replaced by the word "was."
   C. The word "suppose" should be replaced by the word "supposed."
   D. The word "teach" should be replaced by the word "learn."

5. If you had taken my advice; you would have spoken with him. 5.____
   A. This is an example of good formal English usage.
   B. The word "advice" should be spelled "advise."
   C. The words "had taken" should be replaced by the word "take."
   D. The semicolon should be changed to a comma.

KEY (CORRECT ANSWERS)

1. C
2. D
3. A
4. C
5. D

TEST 2

DIRECTIONS: Select the correct answer. *PRINT THE LETTER OF THE CORRECT ANSWER IN THE SPACE AT THE RIGHT.*

1. The one of the following sentences which is MOST acceptable from the viewpoint of correct grammatical usage is:
    A. I do not know which action will have worser results.
    B. He should of known better.
    C. Both the officer on the scene, and his immediate supervisor, is charged with the responsibility.
    D. An officer must have initiative because his supervisor will not always be available to answer questions.

    1.____

2. The one of the following sentences which is MOST acceptable from the viewpoint of correct grammatical usage is:
    A. Of all the officers available, the better one for the job will be picked.
    B. Strict orders were given to all the officers, except he.
    C. Study of the law will enable you to perform your duties more efficiently.
    D. It seems to me that you was wrong in failing to search the two men.

    2.____

3. The one of the following sentences which does NOT contain a misspelled word is:
    A. The duties you will perform are similar to the duties of a patrolman.
    B. Officers must be constantly alert to sieze the initiative.
    C. Officers in this organization are not entitled to special privileges.
    D. Any changes in procedure will be announced publically.

    3.____

4. The one of the following sentences which does NOT contain a misspelled word is:
    A. It will be to your advantage to keep your firearm in good working condition.
    B. There are approximately fourty men on sick leave.
    C. Your first duty will be to pursuade the person to obey the law.
    D. Fires often begin in flameable material kept in lockers.

    4.____

5. The one of the following sentences which does NOT contain a misspelled word is:
    A. Offices are not required to perform technical maintainance.
    B. He violated the regulations on two occasions.
    C. Every employee will be held responable for errors.
    D. This was his nineth absence in a year.

    5.____

KEY (CORRECT ANSWERS)

1. D
2. C
3. C
4. A
5. B

TEST 3

DIRECTIONS: Select the correct answer. *PRINT THE LETTER OF THE CORRECT ANSWER IN THE SPACE AT THE RIGHT.*

1. You are answering a letter that was written on the letterhead of the ABC Company and signed by James H. Wood, Treasurer.
 What is usually considered to be the correct salutation to use in your reply?
 A. Dear ABC Company:
 B. Dear Sirs:
 C. Dear Mr. Wood:
 D. Dear Mr. Treasurer:

 1.____

2. Assume that one of your duties is to handle routine letters of inquiry from the public.
 The one of the following which is usually considered to be MOST desirable in replying to such a letter is a
 A. detailed answer handwritten on the original letter of inquiry
 B. phone call, since you can cover details more easily over the phone than in a letter
 C. short letter giving the specific information requested
 D. long letter discussing all possible aspects of the question raised

 2.____

3. The CHIEF reason for dividing a letter into paragraphs is to
 A. make the message clear to the reader by starting a new paragraph for each new topic
 B. make a short letter occupy as much of the page as possible
 C. keep the reader's attention by providing a pause from time to time
 D. make the letter look neat and businesslike

 3.____

4. Your superior has asked you to send an e-mail from your agency to a government agency in another city. He has written out the message and has indicated the name of the government agency.
 When you dictate the message to your secretary, which of the following items that your superior has NOT mentioned must you be sure to include?
 A. Today's date
 B. The full address of the government agency
 C. A polite opening such as "Dear Sirs"
 D. A final sentence such as "We would appreciate hearing from your agency in reply as soon as is convenient for you"

 4.____

5. The one of the following sentences which is grammatically preferable to the others is:
 A. Our engineers will go over your blueprints so that you may have no problems in construction.
 B. For a long time he had been arguing that we, not he, are to blame for the confusion.
 C. I worked on this automobile for two hours and still cannot find out what is wrong with it.
 D. Accustomed to all kinds of hardships, fatigue seldom bothers veteran policemen.

 5.____

KEY (CORRECT ANSWERS)

1. C
2. C
3. A
4. B
5. A

TEST 4

DIRECTIONS: Select the correct answer. *PRINT THE LETTER OF THE CORRECT ANSWER IN THE SPACE AT THE RIGHT.*

1. Suppose that an applicant for a job as snow laborer presents a letter from a former employer stating: "John Smith has a pleasing manner and never got into an argument with his fellow employees. He was never late or absent."
This letter
   A. indicates that with some training Smith will make a good snow gang boss
   B. presents no definite evidence of Smith's ability to do snow work
   C. proves definitely that Smith has never done any snow work before
   D. proves definitely that Smith will do better than average work as a snow laborer

   1._____

2. Suppose you must write a letter to a local organization in your section refusing a request in connection with collection of their refuse.
You should start the letter by
   A. explaining in detail the consideration you gave the request
   B. praising the organization for its service to the community
   C. quoting the regulation which forbids granting the request
   D. stating your regret that the request cannot be granted

   2._____

3. Suppose a citizen writes in for information as to whether or not he may sweep refuse into the gutter. A Sanitation officer answers as follows:
Dear Sir:
   No person is permitted to litter, sweep, throw or cast, or direct, suffer or permit any person under his control to litter, sweep, throw or cast any ashes, garbage, paper, dust, or other rubbish or refuse into any public street or place, vacant lot, air shaft, areaway, backyard or court.
                              Very truly yours,
                              John Doe
This letter is *poorly* written CHIEFLY because
   A. the opening is not indented   B. the thought is not clear
   C. the tone is too formal and cold D. there are too many commas used

   3._____

4. A section of a disciplinary report written by a Sanitation officer states: "It is requested that subject Sanitation man be advised that his future activities be directed towards reducing his recurrent tardiness else disciplinary action will be initiated which may result in summary discharge."
This section of the report is *poorly* written MAINLY because
   A. at least one word is misspelled   B. it is not simply expressed
   C. more than one idea is expressed   D. the purpose is not stated

   4._____

5. A section of a disciplinary report written by an officer states: "He comes in late. He takes too much time for lunch. He is lazy. I recommend his services be dispensed with."
This section of the report is *poorly* written MAINLY because
   A. it ends with a preposition   B. it is not well organized
   C. no supporting facts are stated   D. the sentences are too simple

   5._____

39

KEY (CORRECT ANSWERS)

1. B
2. D
3. C
4. B
5. C

PREPARING WRITTEN MATERIALS
EXAMINATION SECTION
TEST 1

DIRECTIONS: Each question contains a sentence. Read each sentence carefully to decide whether it is correct. Then, in the space at the right, mark your answer:
   A. If the sentence is incorrect because of bad grammar or sentence structure;
   B. If the sentence is incorrect because of bad punctuation
   C. If the sentence is incorrect because of bad capitalization
   D. If the sentence is correct.

Each incorrect sentence has only one type of error. Consider a sentence correct if it has no errors, although there may be other correct ways of saying the same thing.

SAMPLE QUESTION I: One of our clerks were promoted yesterday.

The subject of this sentence is *one*, so the verb should be *was promoted* instead of *were promoted*. Since the sentence is incorrect because of bad grammar, the answer to Sample Question I is A.

SAMPLE QUESTION II: Between you and me, I would prefer not going there.

Since this sentence is correct, the answer to Sample Question II is D.

1. The National alliance of Businessmen is trying to persuade private businesses to hire youth in the summertime.   1.____

2. The supervisor who is on vacation, is in charge of processing vouchers.   2.____

3. The activity of the committee at its conferences is always stimulating.   3.____

4. After checking the addresses again, the letters went to the mailroom.   4.____

5. The director, as well as the employees, are interested in sharing the dividends.   5.____

6. The experiments conducted by professor Alford were described at a recent meeting of our organization.   6.____

7. I shall be glad to discuss these matters with whoever represents the Municipal Credit Union.   7.____

8. In my opinion, neither Mr. Price nor Mr. Roth knows how to operate this office appliance.   8.____

9. The supervisor, as well as the other stenographers, were unable to transcribe Miss Johnson's shorthand notes.   9.____

10. Important functions such as, recruiting and training, are performed by our unit.   10.____

11. Realizing that many students are interested in this position, we sent announcements to all the High Schools.   11.____

12. After pointing out certain incorrect conclusions, the report was revised by Mr. Clark and submitted to Mr. Batson.   12.____

13. The employer contributed two hundred dollars; the employees, one hundred dollars.   13.____

14. He realized that the time, when a supervisor could hire and fire, was over.   14.____

15. The complaints received by Commissioner Regan was the cause of the change in policy.   15.____

16. Any report, that is to be sent to the Federal Security Administration, must be approved and signed by Mr. Yound.   16.____

17. Of the two stenographers, Miss Rand is the more accurate.   17.____

18. Since the golf courses are crowded during the summer, more men are needed to maintain the courses in good playing condition.   18.____

19. Although he invited Mr. Frankel and I to attend a meeting of the Civil Service Assembly, we were unable to accept his invitation.   19.____

20. Only the employees who worked overtime last week may leave one hour earlier today.   20.____

21. We need someone who can speak french fluently.   21.____

22. A tall, elderly, man entered the office and asked to see Mr. Brown.   22.____

23. The clerk insisted that he had filed the correspondence in the proper cabinet.   23.____

24. "Will you assist us," he asked?   24.____

25. According to the information contained in the report, a large quantity of paper and envelopes were used by this bureau last year   25.____

KEY (CORRECT ANSWERS)

1.	C		11.	C
2.	B		12.	A
3.	D		13.	D
4.	A		14.	B
5.	A		15.	A
6.	C		16.	B
7.	D		17.	D
8.	D		18.	C
9.	A		19.	A
10.	B		20.	D

21. C
22. B
23. D
24. B
25. A

TEST 2

DIRECTIONS: Each question consists of a sentence which may be classified appropriately under one of the following four categories:
- A. Incorrect because of faulty grammar or sentence structure.
- B. Incorrect because of faulty punctuation.
- C. Incorrect because of faulty capitalization.
- D. Correct

Examine each sentence carefully. Then, in the space at the right, print the capital letter preceding the option which is the BEST of the four suggested above. All incorrect sentences contain only one type of error. Consider a sentence correct if it contains none of the types of errors mentioned, although there may be other correct ways of expressing the same thought.

1. Mrs. Black the supervisor of the unit, has many important duties. 1._____
2. We spoke to the man whom you saw yesterday. 2._____
3. When a holiday falls on sunday, it is officially celebrated on monday. 3._____
4. Of the two reports submitted, this one is the best. 4._____
5. Each staff member, including the accountants, were invited to the meeting. 5._____
6. Give the package to whomever calls for it. 6._____
7. To plan the work is our responsibility; to carry it out is his. 7._____
8. "May I see the person in charge of this office," asked the visitor? 8._____
9. He knows that it was not us who prepared the report. 9._____
10. These problems were brought to the attention of senator Johnson. 10._____
11. The librarian classifies all books periodicals and documents. 11._____
12. Any employee who uses an adding machine realizes its importance. 12._____
13. Instead of coming to the office, the clerk should of come to the supply room. 13._____
14. He asked, "will your staff assist us?" 14._____
15. Having been posted on the bulletin board, we were certain that the announcements would be read. 15._____
16. He was not informed, that he would have to work overtime. 16._____
17. The wind blew several paper off of his desk. 17._____

18. Charles Dole, who is a member of the committee, was asked to confer with commissioner Wilson. 18.____

19. Miss Bell will issue a copy to whomever asks for one. 19.____

20. Most employees, and he is no exception do not like to work overtime. 20.____

21. This is the man whom you interviewed last week. 21.____

22. Of the two cities visited, White Plains is the cleanest. 22.____

23. Although he was willing to work on other holidays, he refused to work on Labor day. 23.____

24. If an employee wishes to attend the conference, he should fill out the necessary forms. 24.____

25. The division chief reports that an engineer and an inspector is needed for this special survey. 25.____

KEY (CORRECT ANSWERS)

1.	B		11.	B
2.	D		12.	D
3.	C		13.	A
4.	A		14.	C
5.	A		15.	A
6.	A		16.	B
7.	D		17.	A
8.	B		18.	C
9.	A		19.	A
10.	C		20.	B

21.	D
22.	A
23.	C
24.	D
25.	A

TEST 3

DIRECTIONS: Each question consists of a sentence which may be classified appropriately under one of the following four categories:
- A. Incorrect because of faulty grammar or sentence structure.
- B. Incorrect because of faulty punctuation.
- C. Incorrect because of faulty capitalization.
- D. Correct

Examine each sentence carefully. Then, in the space at the right, print the capital letter preceding the option which is the BEST of the four suggested above. All incorrect sentences contain only one type of error. Consider a sentence correct if it contains none of the types of errors mentioned, although there may be other correct ways of expressing the same thought.

1. We have learned that there was more than twelve people present at the meeting.   1._____

2. Every one of the employees is able to do this kind of work.   2._____

3. Neither the supervisor nor his assistant are in the office today.   3._____

4. The office manager announced that any clerk, who volunteered for the assignment, would be rewarded.   4._____

5. After looking carefully in all the files, the letter was finally found on a desk.   5._____

6. In answer to the clerk's question, the supervisor said, "this assignment must be completed today."   6._____

7. The office manager says that he can permit only you and me to go to the meeting.   7._____

8. The supervisor refused to state who he would assign to the reception unit.   8._____

9. At the last meeting, he said that he would interview us in september.   9._____

10. Mr. Jones, who is one of our most experienced employees has been placed in charge of the main office.   10._____

11. I think that this adding machine is the most useful of the two we have in our office.   11._____

12. Between you and I, our new stenographer is not as competent as our former stenographer.   12._____

13. The new assignment should be given to whoever can do the work rapidly   13._____

14. Mrs. Smith, as well as three other typists, was assigned to the new office.   14._____

15. The staff assembled for the conference on time but, the main speaker arrived late. 15.____

16. The work was assigned to Miss Green and me. 16.____

17. The staff regulations state that an employee, who is frequently tardy, may receive a negative evaluation. 17.____

18. He is the kind of person who is always willing to undertake difficult assignments. 18.____

19. Mr. Wright's request cannot be granted under no conditions. 19.____

20. George Colt a new employee, was asked to deliver the report to the Domestic Relations Court. 20.____

21. The supervisor entered the room and said, "The work must be completed today." 21.____

22. The employees were given their assignments and, they were asked to begin work immediately. 22.____

23. The letter will be sent to the United States senate this week. 23.____

24. When the supervisor entered the room, he noticed that the book was laying on the desk. 24.____

25. The price of the pens were higher than the price of the pencils. 25.____

KEY (CORRECT ANSWERS)

1.	A		11.	A
2.	D		12.	A
3.	A		13.	D
4.	B		14.	D
5.	A		15.	B
6.	C		16.	D
7.	D		17.	B
8.	A		18.	D
9.	C		19.	A
10.	B		20.	B

21. D
22. B
23. C
24. A
25. A

———

PREPARING WRITTEN MATERIALS
EXAMINATION SECTION
TEST 1

DIRECTIONS: Each question consists of a sentence which may be classified appropriately under one of the following four categories:
- A. Incorrect because of faulty grammar or sentence structure;
- B. Incorrect because of faulty punctuation;
- C. Incorrect because of faulty capitalization;
- D. Correct

Examine each sentence carefully. Then, in the space at the right, indicate the letter preceding the category which is the BEST of the four suggested above. Each incorrect sentence contains only one type of error. Consider a sentence correct if it contains no errors, although there may be other correct ways of expressing the same thought.

1. All the employees, in this office, are over twenty-one years old. 1._____

2. Neither the clerk nor the stenographer was able to explain what had happened. 2._____

3. Mr. Johnson did not know who he would assign to type the order. 3._____

4. Mr. Marshall called her to report for work on Saturday. 4._____

5. He might of arrived on time if the train has not been delayed. 5._____

6. Some employees on the other hand, are required to fill out these forms every month. 6._____

7. The supervisor issued special instructions to his subordinates to prevent their making errors. 7._____

8. Our supervisor Mr. Williams, expects to be promoted in about two weeks. 8._____

9. We were informed that prof. Morgan would attend the conference. 9._____

10. The clerks were assigned to the old building; the stenographers, to the new building. 10._____

11. The supervisor asked Mr. Smith and I to complete the work as quickly as possible. 11._____

12. He said, that before an employee can be permitted to leave, the report must be finished. 12._____

13. A calculator, in addition to the three computers, are needed in the new office.   13._____

14. Having made many errs in her work, the supervisor asked the typist to be more careful.   14._____

15. "If you are given an assignment," he said, "you should begin work on it as quickly as possible."   15._____

16. All the clerks, including those who have been appointed recently are required to work on the new assignment.   16._____

17. The office manager asked each employee to work one Saturday a month.   17._____

18. Neither Mr. Smith nor Mr. Jones was able to finish his assignment on time.   18._____

19. The task of filing these cards is to be divided equally between you and he.   19._____

20. He is an employee whom we consider to be efficient.   20._____

21. I believe that the new employees are not as punctual as us.   21._____

22. The employees, working in this office, are to be congratulated for their work.   22._____

23. The delay in preparing the report was caused, in his opinion, by the lack of proper supervision and coordination.   23._____

24. John Jones accidentally pushed the wrong button and then all the lights went out.   24._____

25. The investigator ought to of had the witness sign the statement.   25._____

KEY (CORRECT ANSWERS)

1.	B	11.	A
2.	D	12.	B
3.	A	13.	A
4.	C	14.	A
5.	A	15.	D
6.	B	16.	B
7.	D	17.	C
8.	B	18.	D
9.	C	19.	A
10.	D	20.	D

21. A
22. B
23. D
24. D
25. A

TEST 2

Questions 1-10.

DIRECTIONS: Each of the following sentences may be classified under one of the following four options:
- A. Faulty; contains an error in grammar only
- B. Faulty; contains an error in spelling only
- C. Faulty; contains an error in grammar and an error in spelling
- D. Correct; contains no error in grammar or in spelling

Examine each sentence carefully to determine under which of the above four options it is BEST classified. Then, in the space at the right, write the letter preceding the option which is the best of the four listed above.

1. A recognized principle of good management is that an assignment should be given to whomever is best qualified to carry it out. 1._____

2. He considered it a privilege to be allowed to review and summarize the technical reports issued annually by your agency. 2._____

3. Because the warehouse was in an inaccessible location, deliveries of electric fixtures from the warehouse were made only in large lots. 3._____

4. Having requisitioned the office supplies, Miss Brown returned to her desk and resumed the computation of petty cash disbursements. 4._____

5. One of the advantages of this chemical solution is that records treated with it are not inflamable. 5._____

6. The complaint of this employee, in addition to the complaints of the other employees, were submitted to the grievance committee. 6._____

7. A study of the duties and responsibilities of each of the various categories of employees was conducted by an unprejudiced classification analyst. 7._____

8. Ties of friendship with this subordinate compels him to withold the censure that the subordinate deserves. 8._____

9. Neither of the agencies are affected by the decision to institute a program for rehabilitating physically handi-caped men and women. 9._____

10. The chairman stated that the argument between you and he was creating an intolerable situation. 10._____

Questions 11-25.

DIRECTIONS: Each of the following sentences may be classified under one of the following four options:
- A. Correct
- B. Sentence contains an error in spelling
- C. Sentence contains an error in grammar
- D. Sentence contains errors in both grammar and spelling.

11. He reported that he had had a really good time during his vacation although the farm was located in a very inaccessible portion of the country.   11.____

12. It looks to me like he has been fasinated by that beautiful painting.   12.____

13. We have permitted these kind of pencils to accumulate on our shelves, knowing we can sell them at a profit of five cents apiece any time we choose.   13.____

14. Believing that you will want an unexagerated estimate of the amount of business we can expect, I have made every effort to secure accurate figures.   14.____

15. Each and every man, woman and child in that untrammeled wilderness carry guns for protection against the wild animals.   15.____

16. Although this process is different than the one to which he is accustomed, a good chemist will have no trouble.   16.____

17. Insensible to the fuming and fretting going on about him, the engineer continued to drive the mammoth dynamo to its utmost capacity.   17.____

18. Everyone had studied his lesson carefully and was consequently well prepared when the instructor began to discuss the fourth dimention.   18.____

19. I learned Johnny six new arithmetic problems this afternoon.   19.____

20. Athletics is urged by our most prominent citizens as the pursuit which will enable the younger generation to achieve that ideal of education, a sound mind in a sound body.   20.____

21. He did not see whoever was at the door very clearly but thinks it was the city tax appraiser.   21.____

22. He could not scarsely believe that his theories had been substantiated in this convincing fashion.   22.____

23. Although you have displayed great ingenuity in carrying out your assignments, the choice for the position still lies among Brown and Smith.   23.____

3 (#2)

24. If they had have pleaded at the time that Smith was an accessory to the crime, it would have lessened the punishment.   24.____

25. It has proven indispensible in his compilation of the facts in the matter.   25.____

KEY (CORRECT ANSWERS)

1.	A	11.	A
2.	D	12.	D
3.	B	13.	C
4.	D	14.	B
5.	B	15.	D
6.	A	16.	C
7.	D	17.	A
8.	C	18.	B
9.	C	19.	C
10.	A	20.	A

21.	B
22.	D
23.	C
24.	D
25.	B

TEST 3

Questions 1-5.

DIRECTIONS: Questions 1 through 5 consist of sentences which may or may not contain errors in grammar or spelling or both. Sentences which do not contain errors in grammar or spelling or both are to be considered correct, even though there may be other correct ways of expressing the same thought. Examine each sentence carefully. Then, in the space at the right, write the letter of the answer which is the BEST of those suggested below.
- A. If the sentence is correct
- B. If the sentence contains an error in spelling
- C. If the sentence contains an error in grammar
- D. If the sentence contains errors in both grammar and spelling.

1. Brown is doing fine although the work is irrevelant to his training. 1.____

2. The conference of sales managers voted to set its adjournment at one o'clock in order to give those present an opportunity to get rid of all merchandise. 2.____

3. He decided that in view of what had taken place at the hotel that he ought to stay and thank the benificent stranger who had rescued him from an embarassing situation. 3.____

4. Since you object to me criticizing your letter, I have no alternative but to consider you a mercenary scoundrel. 4.____

5. I rushed home ahead of schedule so that you will leave me go to the picnic with Mary. 5.____

Questions 6-15.

DIRECTIONS: Some of the following sentences contain an error in spelling, word usage, or sentence structure, or punctuation. Some sentences are correct as they stand although there may be other correct ways of expressing the same thought. All incorrect sentences contain only one error. Mark your answer to each question in the space at the right as follows:
- A. If the sentence has an error in spelling
- B. If the sentence has an error in punctuation or capitalization
- C. If the sentence has an error in word usage or sentence structure
- D. If the sentence is correct

6. Because the chairman failed to keep the participants from wandering off into irrelevant discussions, it was impossible to reach a consensus before the meeting was adjourned. 6.____

7. Certain employers have an unwritten rule that any applicant, who is over 55 years of age, is automatically excluded from consideration for any position whatsoever. 7.____

55

8. If the proposal to build schools in some new apartment buildings were to be accepted by the builders, one of the advantages that could be expected to result would be better communication between teachers and parents of schoolchildren.   8._____

9. In this instance, the manufacturer's violation of the law against deseptive packaging was discernible only to an experienced inspector.   9._____

10. The tenants' anger stemmed from the president's going to Washington to testify without consulting them first.   10._____

11. Did the president of this eminent banking company say; "We intend to hire and train a number of these disadvantaged youths?"   11._____

12. In addition, today's confidential secretary must be knowledgable in many different areas: for example, she must know modern techniques for making travel arrangements for the executive.   12._____

13. To avoid further disruption of work in the offices, the protesters were forbidden from entering the building unless they had special passes.   13._____

14. A valuable secondary result of our training conferences is the opportunities afforded for management to observe the reactions of the participants.   14._____

15. Of the two proposals submitted by the committee, the first one is the best.   15._____

Questions 16-25.

DIRECTIONS: Each of the following sentences may be classified MOST appropriately under one of the following three categories:
  A. Faulty because of incorrect grammar
  B. Faulty because of incorrect punctuation
  C. Correct

Examine each sentence. Then, print the capital letter preceding the BEST choice of the three suggested above. All incorrect sentences contain only one type of error. Consider a sentence correct if it contains none of the types of errors mentioned, even though there may be other ways of expressing the same thought.

16. He sent the notice to the clerk who you hired yesterday.   16._____

17. It must be admitted, however that you were not informed of this change.   17._____

18. Only the employees who have served in this grade for at least two years are eligible for promotion.   18._____

19. The work was divided equally between she and Mary.   19._____

3 (#3)

20. He thought that you were not available at that time.   20._____

21. When the messenger returns; please give him this package.   21._____

22. The new secretary prepared, typed, addressed, and delivered, the notices. 22._____

23. Walking into the room, his desk can be seen at the rear.   23._____

24. Although John has worked here longer than she, he produces a smaller   24._____
    amount of work.

25. She said she could of typed this report yesterday.   25._____

KEY (CORRECT ANSWERS)

1.	D	11.	B
2.	A	12.	A
3.	D	13.	C
4.	C	14.	D
5.	C	15.	C
6.	A	16.	A
7.	B	17.	B
8.	D	18.	C
9.	A	19.	A
10.	D	20.	C

21.	B
22.	B
23.	A
24.	C
25.	A

TEST 4

Questions 1-5.

DIRECTIONS: Each of the following sentences may be classified MOST appropriately under one of the following three categories:
- A. Faulty because of incorrect grammar
- B. Faulty because of incorrect punctuation
- C. Correct

Examine each sentence. Then, print the capital letter preceding the BEST choice of the three suggested above. All incorrect sentences contain only one type of error. Consider a sentence correct if it contains none of the types of errors mentioned, even though there may be other ways of expressing the same thought.

1. Neither one of these procedures are adequate for the efficient performance of this task. 1.____

2. The keyboard is the tool of the typist; the cash register, the tool of the cashier. 2.____

3. "The assignment must be completed as soon as possible" said the supervisor. 3.____

4. As you know, office handbooks are issued to all new employees. 4.____

5. Writing a speech is sometimes easier than to deliver it before an audience. 5.____

Questions 6-15.

DIRECTIONS: Each statement given in Questions 6 through 15 contains one of the faults of English usage listed below. For each, choose from the options listed the MAJOR fault contained.
- A. The statement is not a complete sentence.
- B. The statement contains a word or phrase that is redundant.
- C. The statement contains a long, less commonly used word when a shorter, more direct word would be acceptable.
- D. The statement contains a colloquial expression that normally is avoided in business writing.

6. The fact that this activity will afford an opportunity to meet your group. 6.____

7. Do you think that the two groups can join together for next month's meeting? 7.____

8. This is one of the most exciting new innovations to be introduced into our college. 8.____

9. We expect to consummate the agenda before the meeting ends tomorrow at noon.   9.____

10. While this seminar room is small in size, we think we can use it.   10.____

11. Do you think you can make a modification in the date of the Budget Committee meeting?   11.____

12. We are cognizant of the problem but we think we can ameliorate the situation.   12.____

13. Shall I call you around three on the day I arrive in the City?   13.____

14. Until such time that we know precisely that the students will be present.   14.____

15. The consensus of opinion of all the members present is reported in the minutes.   15.____

Questions 16-25.

DIRECTIONS: For each of Questions 16 through 25, select from the options given below the MOST applicable choice.
   A. The sentence is correct.
   B. The sentence contains a spelling error only.
   C. The sentence contains an English grammar error only.
   D. The sentence contains both a spelling error and an English grammar error.

16. Every person in the group is going to do his share.   16.____

17. The man who we selected is new to this University.   17.____

18. She is the older of the four secretaries on the two staffs that are to be combined.   18.____

19. The decision has to be made between him and I.   19.____

20. One of the volunteers are too young for his complicated task, don't you think?   20.____

21. I think your idea is splindid and it will improve this report considerably.   21.____

22. Do you think this is an exagerated account of the behavior you and me observed this morning?   22.____

23. Our supervisor has a clear idea of excelence.   23.____

24. How many occurences were verified by the observers?   24.____

25. We must complete the typing of the draft of the questionaire by noon tomorrow.

25._____

KEY (CORRECT ANSWERS)

1.	A	11.	C
2.	C	12.	C
3.	B	13.	D
4.	C	14.	A
5.	A	15.	B
6.	A	16.	A
7.	B	17.	C
8.	B	18.	C
9.	C	19.	C
10.	B	20.	D

21.	B
22.	D
23.	B
24.	B
25.	B

PREPARING WRITTEN MATERIAL
EXAMINATION SECTION
TEST 1

DIRECTIONS: Each question consists of a sentence which may or may not be an example of good English usage. Examine each sentence, considering grammar, punctuation, spelling, capitalization, and awkwardness. Then choose the correct statement about it from the four choices below it. If the English usage in the sentence given is better than any of the changes suggested in choices B, C, or D, pick choice A. (Do not pick a choice that will change the meaning of the sentence.) *PRINT THE LETTER OF THE CORRECT ANSWER IN THE SPACE AT THE RIGHT.*

1. We attended a staff conference on Wednesday the new safety and fire rules were discussed. 1.____
    A. This is an example of acceptable writing.
    B. The words "safety," "fire," and "rules" should begin with capital letters.
    C. There should be a comma after the word "Wednesday."
    D. There should be a period after the word "Wednesday" and the word "the" should begin with a capital letter.

2. Neither the dictionary or the telephone directory could be found in the office library. 2.____
    A. This is an example of acceptable writing.
    B. The word "or" should be changed to "nor."
    C. The word "library" should be spelled "libery."
    D. The word "neither" should be changed to "either."

3. The report would have been typed correctly if the typist could read the draft. 3.____
    A. This is an example of acceptable writing.
    B. The word "would" should be removed.
    C. The word "have" should be inserted after the word "could."
    D. The word "correctly" should be changed to "correct."

4. The supervisor brought the reports and forms to an employees desk. 4.____
    A. This is an example of acceptable writing.
    B. The word "brought" should be changed to "took."
    C. There should be a comma after the word "reports" and a comma after the word "forms."
    D. The word "employees" should be spelled "employee's."

5. It's important for all the office personnel to submit their vacation schedules on time. 5.____
    A. This is an example of acceptable writing.
    B. The word "It's" should be spelled "Its."
    C. The word "their" should be spelled "they're."
    D. The word "personnel" should be spelled "personal."

6. The report, along with the accompanying documents, were submitted for review. 6._____
   A. This is an example of acceptable writing.
   B. The words "were submitted" should be changed to "was submitted."
   C. The word "accompanying" should be spelled "accompaning."
   D. The comma after the word "report" should be taken out.

7. If others must use your files, be certain that they understand how the system works, but insist that you do all the filing and refiling. 7._____
   A. This is an example of acceptable writing.
   B. There should be a period after the word "works," and the word "but" should start a new sentence.
   C. The words "filing" and "refiling" should be spelled "fileing" and "refileing."
   D. There should be a comma after the word "but."

8. The appeal was not considered because of its late arrival. 8._____
   A. This is an example of acceptable writing.
   B. The word "its" should be changed to "it's."
   C. The word "its" should be changed to "the."
   D. The words "late arrival" should be changed to "arrival late."

9. The letter must be read carefuly to determine under which subject it should be filed. 9._____
   A. This is an example of acceptable writing.
   B. The word "under" should be changed to "at."
   C. The word "determine" should be spelled "determin."
   D. The word "carefuly" should be spelled "carefully."

10. He showed potential as an office manager, but he lacked skill in delegating work. 10._____
    A. This is an example of acceptable writing.
    B. The word "delegating" should be spelled "delagating."
    C. The word "potential" should be spelled "potencial."
    D. The words "he lacked" should be changed to "was lacking."

KEY (CORRECT ANSWERS)

1.	D	6.	B
2.	B	7.	A
3.	C	8.	A
4.	D	9.	D
5.	A	10.	A

TEST 2

DIRECTIONS: Each question consists of a sentence which may or may not be an example of good English usage. Examine each sentence, considering grammar, punctuation, spelling, capitalization, and awkwardness. Then choose the correct statement about it from the four choices below it. If the English usage in the sentence given is better than any of the changes suggested in choices B, C, or D, pick choice A. (Do not pick a choice that will change the meaning of the sentence.) *PRINT THE LETTER OF THE CORRECT ANSWER IN THE SPACE AT THE RIGHT.*

1. The supervisor wants that all staff members report to the office at 9:00 A.M.
   A. This is an example of acceptable writing.
   B. The word "that" should be removed and the word "to" should be inserted after the word "members."
   C. There should be a comma after the word "wants" and a comma after the word "office."
   D. The word "wants" should be changed to "want" and the word "shall" should be inserted after the word "members."

2. Every morning the clerk opens the office mail and distributes it.
   A. This is an example of acceptable writing.
   B. The word "opens" should be changed to "open."
   C. The word "mail" should be changed to "letters."
   D. The word "it" should be changed to "them."

3. The secretary typed more fast on a desktop computer than on a laptop computer.
   A. This is an example of acceptable writing.
   B. The words "more fast" should be changed to "faster."
   C. There should be a comma after the words "desktop computer."
   D. The word "than" should be changed to "then."

4. The new stenographer needed a desk a computer, a chair and a blotter.
   A. This is an example of acceptable writing.
   B. The word "blotter" should be spelled "blodder."
   C. The word "stenographer" should begin with a capital letter.
   D. There should be a comma after the word "desk."

5. The recruiting officer said, "There are many different goverment jobs available."
   A. This is an example of acceptable writing.
   B. The word "There" should not be capitalized.
   C. The word "government" should be spelled "government."
   D. The comma after the word "said" should be removed.

6. He can recommend a mechanic whose work is reliable.
   A. This is an example of acceptable writing.
   B. The word "reliable" should be spelled "relyable."
   C. The word "whose" should be spelled "who's."
   D. The word "mechanic should be spelled "mecanic."

63

7. She typed quickly; like someone who had not a moment to lose. 7._____
   A. This is an example of acceptable writing.
   B. The word "not" should be removed.
   C. The semicolon should be changed to a comma.
   D. The word "quickly" should be placed before instead of after the word "typed."

8. She insisted that she had to much work to do. 8._____
   A. This is an example of acceptable writing.
   B. The word "insisted" should be spelled "incisted."
   C. The word "to" used in front of "much" should be spelled "too."
   D. The word "do" should be changed to "be done."

9. He excepted praise from his supervisor for a job well done. 9._____
   A. This is an example of acceptable writing.
   B. The word "excepted" should be spelled "accepted."
   C. The order of the words "well done" should be changed to "done well."
   D. There should be a comma after the word "supervisor."

10. What appears to be intentional errors in grammar occur several times in the passage. 10._____
    A. This is an example of acceptable writing.
    B. The word "occur" should be spelled "occurr."
    C. The word "appears" should be changed to "appear."
    D. The phrase "several times" should be changed to "from time to time."

KEY (CORRECT ANSWERS)

1. B   6. A
2. A   7. C
3. B   8. C
4. D   9. B
5. C   10. C

TEST 3

DIRECTIONS: Each question consists of a sentence which may or may not be an example of good English usage. Examine each sentence, considering grammar, punctuation, spelling, capitalization, and awkwardness. Then choose the correct statement about it from the four choices below it. If the English usage in the sentence given is better than any of the changes suggested in choices B, C, or D, pick choice A. (Do not pick a choice that will change the meaning of the sentence.) *PRINT THE LETTER OF THE CORRECT ANSWER IN THE SPACE AT THE RIGHT.*

1. The clerk could have completed the assignment on time if he knows where these materials were located.
    A. This is an example of acceptable writing.
    B. The word "knows" should be replaced by "had known."
    C. The word "were" should be replaced by "had been."
    D. The words "where these materials were located" should be replaced by "the location of these materials."

1.____

2. All employees should be given safety training. Not just those who accidents.
    A. This is an example of acceptable writing.
    B. The period after the word "training" should be changed to a colon.
    C. The period after the word "training" should be changed to a semicolon, and the first letter of the word "Not" should be changed to a small "n."
    D. The period after the word "training" should be changed to a comma, and the first letter of the word "Not" should be changed to a small "n."

2.____

3. This proposal is designed to promote employee awareness of the suggestion program, to encourage employee participation in the program, and to increase the number of suggestions submitted.
    A. This is an example of acceptable writing.
    B. The word "proposal" should be spelled "proposal."
    C. The words "to increase the number of suggestions submitted" should be changed to "an increase in the number of suggestions is expected."
    D. The word "promote" should be changed to "enhance" and the word "increase" should be changed to "add to."

3.____

4. The introduction of inovative managerial techniques should be preceded by careful analysis of the specific circumstances and conditions in each department.
    A. This is an example of acceptable writing.
    B. The word "technique" should be spelled "techneques."
    C. The word "inovative" should be spelled "innovative."
    D. A comma should be placed after the word "circumstances" and after the word "conditions."

4.____

5. This occurrence indicates that such criticism embarrasses him.   5.____
    A. This is an example of acceptable writing.
    B. The word "occurrence" should be spelled "occurence."
    C. The word "criticism" should be spelled "critisism.
    D. The word "embarrasses" should be spelled "embarasses.

KEY (CORRECT ANSWERS)

1. B
2. D
3. A
4. C
5. A

PREPARING WRITTEN MATERIAL

PARAGRAPH REARRANGEMENT
COMMENTARY

The sentences that follow are in scrambled order. You are to rearrange them in proper order and indicate the letter choice containing the correct answer at the space at the right.

Each group of sentences in this section is actually a paragraph presented in scrambled order. Each sentence in the group has a place in that paragraph; no sentence is to be left out. You are to read each group of sentences and decide upon the best order in which to put the sentences so as to form a well-organized paragraph.

The questions in this section measure the ability to solve a problem when all the facts relevant to its solution are not given.

More specifically, certain positions of responsibility and authority require the employee to discover connection between events sometimes, apparently, unrelated. In order to do this, the employee will find it necessary to correctly infer that unspecified events have probably occurred or are likely to occur. This ability becomes especially important when action must be taken on incomplete information.

Accordingly, these questions require competitors to choose among several suggested alternatives, each of which presents a different sequential arrangement of the events. Competitors must choose the MOST logical of the suggested sequences.

In order to do so, they may be required to draw on general knowledge to infer missing concepts or events that are essential to sequencing the given events. Competitors should be careful to infer only what is essential to the sequence. The plausibility of the wrong alternatives will always require the inclusion of unlikely events or of additional chains of events which are NOT essential to sequencing the given events.

It's very important to remember that you are looking for the best of the four possible choices, and that the best choice of all may not even be one of the answers you're given to choose from.

There is no one right way to solve these problems. Many people have found it helpful to first write out the order of the sentences, as they would have arranged them, on their scrap paper before looking at the possible answers. If their optimum answer is there, this can save them some time. If it isn't, this method can still give insight into solving the problem. Others find it most helpful to just go through each of the possible choices, contrasting each as they go along. You should use whatever method feels comfortable and works for you.

While most of these types of questions are not that difficult, we've added a higher percentage of the difficult type, just to give you more practice. Usually there are only one or two questions on this section that contain such subtle distinctions that you're unable to answer confidently. And you then may find yourself stuck deciding between two possible choices, neither of which you're sure about.

PREPARING WRITTEN MATERIAL
PARAGRAPH REARRANGEMENT
EXAMINATION SECTION
TEST 1

DIRECTIONS: The sentences listed below are part of a meaningful paragraph, but they are not given in their proper order. You are to decide what would be the BEST order to put sentences to form a well-organized paragraph. Each sentence has a place in the paragraph; there are no extra sentences. *PRINT THE LETTER OF THE CORRECT ANSWER IN THE SPACE AT THE RIGHT.*

1. I. At first, I had very low enrollment, but then I started passing out flyers describing my services.
    II. Last summer I started a carwashing venture.
    III. I hope to save enough to buy my own carwash business one day.
    IV. I've been in business almost a year.
    V. After the advertising, I was booked every weekend during the summer.
    The CORRECT answer is:
    A. II, I, V, IV, III   B. I, II, IV, III, V   C. II, I, IV, V, III   D. V, III, IV, I, II

    1.____

2. I. Yesterday, John had to call work and tell them he wouldn't be able to come in.
    II. She wanted to eat at the new seafood restaurant in town.
    III. Two days ago, John and Sally went to dinner for Sally's birthday.
    IV. However, later John realized the sushi made him sick.
    V. They both tried the sushi and thought it tasted good.
    The CORRECT answer is:
    A. I, V, IV, III, II   B. III, II, V, IV, I   C. III, V, IV, I, II   D. V, IV, III, I, II

    2.____

3. I. Music programs should not be cut when school funds are tight.
    II. Some will argue that music programs are too costly.
    III. According to many experts, music programs have even shown the ability to re-engage student populations who have lost interest in scholastic endeavors.
    IV. There is a direct connection between school improvement and a student's connection to music.
    V. However, there are many different programs to choose from that are not as expensive.
    The CORRECT answer is:
    A. IV, II, V, I, III   B. I, III, IV, II, V   C. II, I, III, IV, V   D. I, IV, III, II, V

    3.____

4. I. The hockey team went undefeated in their tournament.
    II. Because the coach and their parents believed in them, the players played with great confidence.
    III. No one wanted to go home after they won the championship.
    IV. Their coach made them believe they could beat anyone they played.
    V. They were not expected to beat all of the teams in their bracket.
    The CORRECT answer is:
    A. III, II, V, IV, I   B. I, II, III, IV, V   C. I, V, IV, II, III   D. I, IV, V, II, III

    4.____

5. I. The problem started when my alarm clock was set for 6:00 P.M. not 6:00 A.M., so I woke up late.
    II. I guess a neighbor's dog got loose before practice started, so it was delayed and no one notices I was a little tardy.
    III. I rode my bike as fast as I could and thought I was going to be in trouble for sure.
    IV. This morning was crazy because if I was late, I would get cut from the team.
    V. When I got to the field, everyone was standing on the outside of the fence and there were policemen all on the field.
    The CORRECT answer is:
    A. I, IV, III, V, II   B. IV, III, I, II, V   C. I, V, II, III, IV   D. IV, I, III, V, II

6. I. Lastly, do not eat food off of your date's plate unless they have offered it to you first.
    II. Do not tell jokes that aren't funny and especially do not laugh at them yourself.
    III. Remember, there are many ways to screw up a date, but these are the worst ways.
    IV. When on a first date, there are many ways to screw it up, but here are the three worst.
    V. Do not forget to shower and groom yourself before showing up.
    The CORRECT answer is:
    A. IV, V, II, I, III   B. I, V, IV, II, III   C. IV, III, II, I, V   D. V, IV, II, I, III

7. I. We could prevent drunk drivers from harming themselves or others by by providing this service.
    II. Thousands each year die because of accidents caused by drugs or alcohol.
    III. Many are not willing to pay for a taxi and decide to drive themselves home instead.
    IV. While the cost may be a burden to the wallet, it would be small compared to the loss of a loved one because of drunk driving.
    V. Lives could be saved if the town started a free taxi service.
    The CORRECT answer is:
    A. I, III, V, IV, II   B. II, V, III, I, IV   C. II, III, I, V, IV   D. V, III, II, IV, I

8. I. These amazing animals are disappearing at a startling rate.
    II. Do people really want to explain to our grandchildren why they can only see these majestic animals in a book?
    III. Zoos all across the country do not want the Siberian tiger to vanish.
    IV. We can also make donations to charities and sanctuaries that protect the Siberian tiger.
    V. If we write to local governments, we could let them know we demand the preservation of this species.
    The CORRECT answer is:
    A. I, III, V, II, IV   B. V, II, I, III, IV   C. III, I, V, IV, II   D. II, IV, V, I, III

9. I.   Often, they have been described as eating machines, and their design certainly matches perfectly for that activity.
    II. Of all the creatures that live in water, Orcas are the greediest eaters and killers.
    III. As soon as they finish a meal, Orcas are on the prowl for more food.
    IV. Orcas, better known as killer whales, are powerful swimmers, with sleek, muscled, stream-lined bodies.
    V.   They suffer from continual hunger.
    The CORRECT answer is:
    A. II, V, III, I, IV   B. II, III, I, IV, V   C. V, II, III, IV, I   D. I, IV, II, III, V

10. I.   Sleep researchers have recently concluded that high school students need more sleep than they currently get.
    II. In an attempt to aid high school students get more sleep, some schools have delayed start times so students can perform better.
    III. In addition to having difficulty with thinking, students who are sleep deprived often see more stress in their lives because of an increase in stress hormones like cortisol.
    IV. Consistent data has determined that sleep is necessary to help with creating memories and solving complex issues.
    V.   At school, teens have difficulty with complex thought because many of them do not get enough sleep each night.
    The CORRECT answer is:
    A. I, V, III, II, IV   B. IV, III, I, V, II   C. I, IV, V, III, II   D. II, III, V, IV, I

11. I.   It took me twice as long to pack because I was so excited.
    II. That all changed on the last day of school.
    III. Until last year, I had never been out of the state, let alone out of the country.
    IV. My sister decided to take me on a trip to London.
    V.   Now I think I want to be a travel agent, so I can see the world.
    The CORRECT answer is:
    A. II, IV, I, V, III   B. III, II, IV, I, V   C. IV, V, I, III, II   D. III, IV, II, I, V

12. I.   The owner felt that tattoos gave a negative image for the coffee shop.
    II. Furthermore, a clean cut appearance would attract better customers.
    III. Since then, the policy has seen few complaints from residents or employees.
    IV. In 2008, a coffee shop in Billings, Montana instituted a policy that banned employees from having tattoos that can be seen by customers.
    V.   When one of the employees refused to wear a long sleeve shirt to cover up, he was told he could no longer work at the coffee shop.
    The CORRECT answer is:
    A. IV, II, III, I, V   B. V, I, II, IV, III   C. I, II, V, III, IV   D. IV, I, II, V, III

13.
I. Our household might have been described as uncooperative.
II. When the tide was high, she would be standing on the inlet bridge with her waders on.
III. Everything was subservient to the disposal of the tides.
IV. I grew up with buckets, shovels, and nets waiting by the back door.
V. When the tide was low, Mom could be found down on the mudflats.
The CORRECT answer is:
A. I, V, IV, V, III   B. IV, I, III, V, II   C. V, IV, II, I, III   D. II, IV, I, III, V

14.
I. A 2012 survey found that over 50% of those polled thought educators were prohibited from teaching about religion.
II. The result is that many schools and teachers are hesitant to educate students about world religions.
III. However, for many it is impossible to deny the role that religion plays in history and literature.
IV. As many people know, the First Amendment guarantees the separation of church and state.
V. Ultimately, this is a dilemma that will continue to plague Social Studies and World History educators.
The CORRECT answer is:
A. IV, I, III, V, II   B. I, III, V, II, IV   C. IV, III, II, I, V   D. II, III, V, IV, I

15.
I. The Wampanoag religion was similar to that of the other Algonquin tribes.
II. They also had spiritual beliefs about animals, and the forest.
III. Then, they told their stories of the cycle of life and the Great Spirit.
IV. They expressed their religious beliefs during festivals and at night when they sat at huge campfires.
V. In those times, people believed in a Great Spirit and many other things that Nature had a part of the Great Spirit in them.
The CORRECT answer is:
A. I, V, II, IV, III   B. V, II, III, I, IV   C. I, II, III, IV, V   D. III, IV, II, V, I

16.
I. Consumers spend an endless amount of money each year on cutting, lengthening, highlighting and curling hair.
II. Brunettes want to be blonde, redheads long to be brunettes, and all cringe at the thought of gray hair.
III. Why is everyone so obsessed with the hair on their heads?
IV. These thoughts all crossed my mind as I examine the result of my most recent hair adventure.
V. The result was not quite what I expected, but I resolved to live with it, as it's my hair and no one else's!
The CORRECT answer is:
A. I, IV, V, II, III   B. I, III, II, IV, V   C. IV, I, III, V, II   D. III, I, II, IV, V

17.
I. It was only years afterwards that he learned his ancestors were actually accomplished coppersmiths.
II. He's an old-fashioned current day blacksmith that still practices manipulating metal over hot fires.
III. This started him on his quest to collect and read any and every book concerning the nature and process of blacksmithing.
IV. Beginning at age 30, Lee's attraction to metal work lay in creating an object out of such obstinate material such as iron.
V. While one will probably never read about him in a history book, Mr. Amos Lee contributes mightily to the preservation of America.
The CORRECT answer is:
A. II, III, I, IV, V   B. V, II, IV, III, I   C. III, I, V, II, IV   D. I, IV, III, V, II

17._____

18.
I. After she was stung, she killed the scorpion with a boot, and flushed it down the sink.
II. My sister once told me about a scorpion that stung her in her bed.
III. As she recounted her tale of horror, I could only wonder how she remained so calm.
IV. Later, she realized she should've kept it to figure out what type of scorpion it was.
V. While she's lucky to be alive, it could've been a deadly scorpion that would've required medical attention immediately.
The CORRECT answer is:
A. II, III, I, IV, V   B. II, I, IV, V, III   C. I, IV, II, III, V   D. V, II, III, I, IV

18._____

19.
I. While the majority of people know this, it was not always the case.
II. Many laws hold sponsors responsible to participants and courts are full of non-compliance lawsuits on both sides.
III. Seven months after departure, she arrived at her destination, battered and tired, but the contest sponsors were nowhere to be found.
IV. For anyone who has ever entered a contest, the rules and disclaimers that go along with each one are well known.
V. In 1896, a contest motivated a Norwegian immigrant to travel from New York City to the state of Washington.
The CORRECT answer is:
A. II, III, V, IV, I   B. V, I, IV, III, II   C. IV, II, I, V, III   D. I, IV, III, II, V

19._____

20.
I. One thought as to why this happens is due to a person's circadian rhythm being thrown off.
II. While most people find traveling internationally to be exhilarating, those same people would probably agree that the worst part is the jet lag.
III. It is considered a sleeping disorder, albeit one that is temporary and not as serious as other sleeping dysfunctions.
IV. Normally, the body operates on a 24-hour time period in conjunction with the earth's 24-hour cycle of night and day.
V. When one adds or subtracts time while traveling, a condition known as desynchronosis likely affects them.
The CORRECT answer is:
A. I, II, III, IV, V   B. IV, I, III, V, II   C. III, IV, I, II, V   D. II, V, III, I, IV

20._____

21.
   I. The consumption rate is due to its ability to create cleaner fuel for electrical power.
   II. While cleaner burning fuel is optimal, the usage rate will mean the U.S. only has about a five-year supply of natural gas.
   III. Current research studies are showing that Americans use around 20 trillion cubic feet (TCF) on a yearly basis.
   IV. It is no wonder, then, that natural gas has become such a controversial and critical topic for politicians, businesses, and consumers.
   V. While gasoline is still a crucial energy source, natural gas actually supplies approximately one-fourth of America's energy needs.
   The CORRECT answer is:
   A. I, IV, II, III, V   B. IV, II, III, V, I   C. V, III, I, II, IV   D. III, V, IV, I, II

21.____

22.
   I. Their protection comes from bony plates covered by leathery skin.
   II. This desert wanderer has few worries and one can understand why: his "coat" of armor.
   III. What would be certain death for most animals, armadillos meander along highway shoulders and remains surprisingly unaffected.
   IV. While their shells are not impenetrable, the armadillo can relax knowing that he is safer than many animals who wander the roads of the southwest.
   V. While on the smaller side, armadillos are equipped to deal with aggressive and dangerous predators.
   The CORRECT answer is:
   A. III, II, V, I, IV   B. IV, I, II, V, III   C. I, III, IV, II, V   D. V, IV, I, III, II

22.____

23.
   I. Since its discovery in 1930, Pluto has had a troubled history concerning its acceptance as a planet.
   II. Anytime there is a controversial topic like this, it is sure to be debated for years to come.
   III. Some researchers believe that it is a planet arguing that Pluto is almost 1,000 times bigger than an average comet.
   IV. However, others argue that due to its icy composition and irregular orbit, Pluto more likely belongs to the Kuiper Belt, which features sizeable comets.
   V. They also argue that any would be planet must be large enough to be pulled into a spherical shape by its own gravity, which like the other eight, Pluto can lay claim to.
   The CORRECT answer is:
   A. IV, V, I, II, III   B. I, III, V, IV, II   C. III, I, IV, V, II   D. II, IV, V, III, I

23.____

24. I. When I found out I'd be traveling to France, I was so ecstatic.
    II. He told me that studying may be difficult because I will want to meet new friends and see all the landmarks associated with such a beautiful country.
    III. My brother has also been in an exchange before and he had some advice for me.
    IV. Despite his warnings to study hard, I know I would be disappointed if I didn't do any sightseeing at all.
    V. In the fall, I will be participating in a foreign exchange program.
    The CORRECT answer is:
    A. I, V, II, IV, III   B. IV, II, I, III, V   C. III, I, II, IV, IV   D. V, I, III, II, IV

25. I. Well over two hundred years ago, Lewis and Clark set forth on a journey at the request of President Thomas Jefferson.
    II. Their instructions were simple; they needed to find the fastest route across North America.
    III. Throughout it all, including long winters and harsh conditions, the travelers forged west in search of a trade route using only rivers.
    IV. The actual task was much more difficult as it would require them to set a course through dangerous territories replete with hostile natives and ferocious animals.
    V. While land travel ended up being faster, many still credit this group with "breaking through" into the unknown land and launching a movement for westward expansion.
    The CORRECT answer is:
    A. I, II, IV, III, V   B. II, I, III, IV, V   C. V, III, IV, II, I   D. IV, I, III, V, II

KEY (CORRECT ANSWERS)

1.	A	11.	B
2.	B	12.	D
3.	D	13.	B
4.	C	14.	C
5.	D	15.	A
6.	A	16.	D
7.	B	17.	B
8.	C	18.	A
9.	A	19.	C
10.	C	20.	D

21. C
22. A
23. B
24. D
25. A

TEST 2

DIRECTIONS: The sentences listed below are part of a meaningful paragraph, but they are not given in their proper order. You are to decide what would be the BEST order to put sentences to form a well-organized paragraph. Each sentence has a place in the paragraph; there are no extra sentences. *PRINT THE LETTER OF THE CORRECT ANSWER IN THE SPACE AT THE RIGHT.*

1. I. Whenever I start to feel sadness and disgust over a poor hair style, I ask myself why we are so obsessed with the hair on our heads.
    II. The answer always comes to me in a flash.
    III. Soon after this realization, I often cease my crying over how I look.
    IV. It's pure vanity; no other reason explains fully why we worry about how to style, color or cut our follicles.
    V. Instead, I focus on positive, kind thoughts towards myself and others, which usually allows me to overcome any negative feelings I had right after I looked in the mirror.
    The CORRECT answer is:
    A. III, I, V, IV, II   B. I, II, IV, III, V   C. IV, III, II, V, I   D. V, IV, I, II, III

2. I. The riverboat director was our captain and our host.
    II. We affectionately watched him with his back toward us, as he stood at the helm, looking toward the sea.
    III. Within all of the Mississippi River, nothing looked nearly as nautical and trustworthy as our pilot as he surveyed the waters before him.
    IV. What we had not realized at the time was that his work was not out there in the estuaries, but rather behind him, within the gloom of the vessel.
    V. We would realize soon enough, however, how difficult the next few days would get, and why he was so ponderous on that ship deck.
    The CORRECT answer is:
    A. III, I, IV, II, V   B. IV, II, III, V, I   C. V, II, I, IV, III   D. I, III, II, IV, V

3. I. Ultimately, no new qualities are added to an object, person, or action when it becomes good.
    II. Whenever one examines the word "good", there is always an implied end to be reached.
    III. The good is useful, and it must be used for something.
    IV. However, good is a relative term.
    V. So in that light, whether good is spoken out loud or silently assumed, it is a mental exercise to something else that puts all meaning into it.
    The CORRECT answer is:
    A. V, II, I, IV, III   B. III, I, V, II, IV   C. I, V, IV, III, II   D. II, IV, III, V, I

4.
I. There are specific temperature ranges for petroleum gas, kerosene, oil stocks and also residue.
II. Called fractional distillation, the oil is heated and drawn off at different points, which leads to the various products.
III. To start, the oil is heated up to around 600 degrees Celsius, which vaporizes it.
IV. From there, the vapors cool and condense as they move upwards and eventually turn back into liquid and flows into various tanks.
V. Crude oil is refined when it is split into different by-products.
The CORRECT answer is:
 A. II, III, I, V, IV   B. IV, I, IV, III, V   C. V, II, I, III, IV   D. I, IV, II, III, V

5.
I. With that said, x-ray distortion has more than one use regarding planets.
II. The higher "bend" in an x-ray would seemingly indicate a larger planet, while lower bending would most likely mean a smaller planet.
III. Distortion can also help determine how a planet orbits its star.
IV. Releasing x-rays by distant stars can help reveal the presence of planets orbiting these stars.
V. The distortion of the x-rays, which is how scientists would tell if planets are near, would be caused by gravitational pull exerted from planets.
The CORRECT answer is:
 A. IV, V, II, I, III   B. V, IV, III, I, II   C. II, III, I, IV, V   D. I, V, II, III, IV

6.
I. Some feel that this fact reflects the rise of English as an accepted language of business around the world, and, therefore, that foreign languages are lessening in importance.
II. Foreign language instruction is dropping in U.S. public high schools.
III. They feel that this drop is actually a threat to the nation's vitality in what is an ever-increasing multicultural marketplace.
IV. Others feel that the reduction in language study is a U.S. failure to integrate with the rest of the world.
V. The question then becomes this, should greater support be given to foreign language programs in U.S. public schools?
The CORRECT answer is:
 A. V, IV, III, I, II   B. III, IV, V, II, I   C. II, I, IV, III, V   D. IV, II, III, V, I

7.
I. The owner, Nate, still runs the joint, which means it doesn't usually close until he's served the last customer.
II. The alley might dissuade visitors from finding this local gem, but if one can get past the masking tape and yellowing paint that line the door, they will be in for a real treat.
III. The Shack, as the locals call it, is located in a nondescript alley across from beautiful City Park.
IV. While I'd love for Nate to get more publicity, I'm just fine with knowing that the Shack will have a short line and a great ambience each time I stop in.
V. Nathan's Crab Shack serves up some of the best sandwiches I've ever eaten.
The CORRECT answer is:
 A. III, II, V, IV, I   B. I, IV, II, III, V   C. II, V, I, IV, III   D. V, I, III, II, IV

8.
   I. All activity halted, however, at the onset of World War II, so construction did not officially begin until the early 1950s.
   II. In total, it took almost three years to build, cost five men their lives, and cost the state of Michigan more than $40 million.
   III. In the 1930's, the Mackinac Bridge Authority sought funding from the federal government to construct a bridge.
   IV. Even though they were denied, the MBA plotted a route and studied the lake bed and rock below.
   V. Despite numerous setbacks, the Mackinac Bridge opened to traffic on November 1, 1957, and for years it was the longest suspension bridge in the world.
   The CORRECT answer is:
   A. II, I, V, IV, III   B. III, IV, I, II, V   C. V, III, IV, I, II   D. I, II, III, V, IV

   8.____

9.
   I. It also teaches them to bargain and trade for cards to complete their sets.
   II. Collecting cards is a rewarding experience not only for kids, but also adults.
   III. It teaches important skills, such as patience and organization.
   IV. Lastly, card collecting is a social activity that encourages the old and the young to swap stories, cards, and knowledge in a fun and engaging way.
   V. For younger collectors, it enhances fine motor skills such as developing a more careful touch.
   The CORRECT answer is:
   A. III, IV, I, II, V   B. II, V, III, IV, I   C. I, II, V, III, IV   D. II, III, V, I, IV

   9.____

10.
   I. Spyware can cripple unsecured computers and data around the world.
   II. Even when computer users experience program crashes and warnings about missing system files, they tend to wait until these problems get too ad to manage.
   III. Sometimes it is used for marketing agencies, but just as often there is a more malicious intent behind spyware stored on an unsecured computer.
   IV. Much of the time, the cause of these problems rests with the biggest online threat there is: spyware.
   V. While most people do not realize it, those who use a personal computer to connect to the internet expose themselves to many risks.
   The CORRECT answer is:
   A. II, IV, V, III, I   B. V, II, IV, I, III   C. III, II, I, IV, V   D. V, IV, I, II, III

   10.____

11.
   I. When people have parties at their homes, Susan cooks for them, and she is a fabulous cook.
   II. My friend, Susan, owns her own catering business.
   III. Once everything has been planned, Susan will hire servers to wait on the people.
   IV. One of the things that makes her so good is that she asks the customer lots of questions like how many people will be there and what food the customer would like to serve.
   V. All in all, she loves the work involved with her catering business and it does not hurt that she's really good at it.

   11.____

The CORRECT answer is:
A. II, I, IV, III, V   B. I, III, V, II, IV   C. IV, II, I, III, V   D. V, IV, I, III, II

12. I. "To be, or not to be…." is an extremely well-known phrase that has been the source of both mystery and wonderment since the turn of the 16th century.
    II. Where did it come from and what does it mean?
    III. As for the meaning of the phrase, a complete answer would necessitate a deeper, more comprehensive look into Shakespeare culture and nuance.
    IV. The first question is easy enough to answer: from Shakespeare's famous play, *Hamlet*.
    V. The issue, however, is that despite the fact that everyone knows the phrase, few actually know the context of this well-worn saying.
    The CORRECT answer is:
    A. V, I, III, II, IV   B. II, III, IV, V, I   C. I, V, II, IV, III   D. IV, II, I, III, V

13. I. For example, it was recently discovered that we were connected to a Civil War ancestor that we previously had not known about.
    II. He maintains the records of births, deaths, marriages, and even divorces, and he takes the job very seriously.
    III. This ancestor bestowed his beautiful and antique furniture to his children, who then passed the items down to their descendants.
    IV. My Uncle Mike is the genealogist of our family.
    V. In fact, he will even send out letters to our family whenever something noteworthy occurs.
    The CORRECT answer is:
    A. II, III, I, IV, V   B. V, IV, II, III, I   C. I, II, IV, V, III   D. IV, II, V, I, III

14. I. He was part of a team that performed complicated experiments during the 1940s.
    II. However, he is most likely known for his creation of "Murphy's Law."
    III. While many Americans do not know the name Edward Murphy, they owe a considerable debt to this member of the Air Force.
    IV. This somewhat funny observation has actually inspired similar "laws" such as Hofstadter's Law.
    V. This "law" states that "if anything can go wrong, it will."
    The CORRECT answer is:
    A. I, III, V, II, IV   B. III, IV, V, I, II   C. III, I, II, V, IV   D. V, II, IV, I, III

15. I. During winter months, its white coat is ideal to camouflage and the insulation provided by its unbeatable fur lining allows the fox to hunt all winter long.
    II. While this strategy could be fruitful, it also carries risk because of the possibility that the polar bear might consume the fox if it catches it.
    III. One of the Snow Fox's unique traits is the ability to adapt to extreme weather conditions.

IV. When food becomes scarce, the Arctic fox can follow polar bears as they attack seals on the sea ice.
V. Often referred to as the "Snow Fox," the Arctic fox is comparable in size to a domestic cat.
The CORRECT answer is:
A. V, III, I, IV, II   B. II, IV, III, I, V   C. III, I, V, II, IV   D. IV, III, II, V, I

16.
I. The venerable professor, aged 85, encouraged his audience to show compassion for the poor and homeless in the city.
II. Students flocked to hear the returning professor, Dr. Willis, give a speech.
III. He abhors opulence and urges people to be charitable through frugality.
IV. Dr. Willis, a kind and empathetic activist for the poor, spoke to a full auditorium on Tuesday.
V. Much of his work is due to his personal memories stemming from the Great Depression.
The CORRECT answer is:
A. I, II, III, IV, V   B. V, IV, III, II, I   C. III, I, IV, II, V   D. II, IV, I, V, III

17.
I. As some of his friends have noted, this antisocial attitude is an aberration for him, as he is normally quite extroverted and cheerful.
II. Many people have tried to evoke some of his normal geniality, but it has not worked, which is disconcerting.
III. It is now a commonly held belief that the only antidote to Johnny's stressful situation would be complete and total success on his exam.
IV. Upon learning of his pending exam, his roommates have agreed that his current mood is directly correlated to the test.
V. Upon being informed of an upcoming test in statistics, Johnny has started to act aloof and uninterested in social activities.
The CORRECT answer is:
A. I, V, II, III, IV   B. IV, III, I, V, II   C. II, IV, I, III, V   D. V, I, IV, II, III

18.
I. When viewing a star formation through the Spitzer Space Telescope, a person has a view of disruption.
II. The Spitzer Space Telescope challenges the commonly held thought that smooth gas clouds gracefully facilitate the creation of new stars.
III. The relative few stars can be attributed to the turbulence that these processes bring to the heavens.
IV. Through the telescope's lens, one can see the creation of a star that disrupts nearby space.
V. Recent models of star formation, aided by telescopes like Spitzer, recognize that stars interact with one another in their stellar neighborhood.
The CORRECT answer is:
A. IV, II, I, III, V   B. I, IV, II, V, III   C. III, I, V, IV, II   D. II, V, III, I, IV

19. I.   In addition, models predicting the placement of electrons within the cloud describe one probability among many, instead of showing planet-like electrons orbiting a sun-like nucleus.
     II. Although the majority of us think of an atom's nucleus being orbited by electrons, the reality differs considerably from the stereotypical depiction.
     III. Oddly enough, it is mostly composed of empty space: its nucleus, made of protons and neutrons, makes up only about a billionth of the atom itself.
     IV. As many people know, the atom is the basic building block of matter.
     V.   Researchers prefer to describe the electron movement as a "wave-pattern cloud."
     The CORRECT answer is:
     A. III, I, V, IV, II   B. V, III, IV, I, II   C. IV, III, II, V, I   D. II, V, I, III, IV

20. I.   These buildings were thought to have been constructed upwards in order to thwart would-be attackers.
     II. Ancient Yemeni architects created a walled city that they called Shibam.
     III. Nowadays, with the planning of mile-high skyscrapers planned for construction, Shibam does not seem as impressive, but given their tools and knowledge at the time, the city will be held in esteem in architecturfal history books.
     IV. This wonder of the old world is now dubbed "Manhattan of the Desert".
     V.   The city was composed of 500 buildings, ranging from five to eight stories high.
     The CORRECT answer is:
     A. II, IV, V, I, III   B. V, III, I, IV, II   C. IV, V, II, III, I   D. III, I, IV, II, V

21. I.   Almost 2,000 years after being buried by falling ash from a volcanic eruption, the residents of Pompeii do reveal fascinating details about daily life in the Roman Empire.
     II. Pompeii's population, roughly 20,000 inhabitants, practiced several different religions.
     III. This is evidenced by temples dedicated to Egyptian gods, as well as Jewish temples and worshippers of Cybele.
     IV. While radically different in beliefs, Pompeii's citizens practiced all of these religions in peaceful co-existence with followers of the state religion.
     V.   These people worshipped Jupiter and the Roman emperor.
     The CORRECT answer is:
     A. I, III, V, II, IV   B. II, IV, I, III, V   C. IV, I, III, V, II   D. III, II, IV, I, V

22.
I. Instead of driving there, I may just stay home and cook myself a big breakfast with toast, fruit, eggs, and bacon.
II. I was going to take a jog around the neighborhood to train for my race.
III. As I woke up today, I realized that it would be yet another rainy day.
IV. Now, I will have to drive to the gymnasium that is on the opposite side of town.
V. After I eat, hopefully the rain will have gone away so I can train successfully.
The CORRECT answer is:
A. IV, I, II, V, III   B. III, II, IV, I, V   C. II, IV, I, III, V   D. V, III, II, I, IV

22.____

23.
I. Yesterday, he received a call from an H.R. representative of a firm in Chicago.
II. The H.R. rep asked William to fly out to Chicago for an interview and he even offered to pay for William's plane ticket.
III. Having received such a generous offer, William could not say no to the interview.
IV. The interview will take place in one week, so William will spend the next few days researching the company's history.
V. William has been searching for a full-time job for the last few months.
The CORRECT answer is:
A. IV, II, III, I, V   B. V, II, I, IV, III   C. I, II, III, IV, V   D. V, I, II, III, IV

23.____

24.
I. I wonder when I'll feel well enough to go back to work.
II. I've tried eating chicken soup, drinking orange juice, taking Benadryl since the weekend.
III. I finally decided to visit the doctor to see if I can get any stronger medicine to help me.
IV. My allergies have been terrible the last several days.
V. I've been blowing my nose, sneezing, and coughing the entire time.
The CORRECT answer is:
A. V, II, IV, III, I   B. I, III, II, IV, V   C. IV, V, II, III, I   D. II, III, V, I, IV

24.____

25.
I. Myrta is a sophomore in college and she's working on her degree in Special Education.
II. In order to prepare herself for her career, she works at a camp in the summer.
III. All of the children who attend this camp have physical and mental disabilities.
IV. Myrta helps the kids get exercise and increase their social skills.
V. At the end of each summer, she cannot wait to start her career in Special Education.
The CORRECT answer is:
A. V, I, II, III, IV   B. I, II, III, IV, V   C. III, IV, V, I, II   D. V, IV, III, II, I

25.____

KEY (CORRECT ANSWERS)

1.	B		11.	A
2.	A		12.	C
3.	D		13.	D
4.	C		14.	C
5.	A		15.	A
6.	C		16.	D
7.	D		17.	D
8.	B		18.	B
9.	D		19.	C
10.	B		20.	A

21. A
22. B
23. D
24. C
25. B

PREPARING WRITTEN MATERIAL
PARAGRAPH REARRANGEMENT

EXAMINATION SECTION
TEST 1

DIRECTIONS: The sentences listed below are part of a meaningful paragraph, but they are not given in their proper order. You are to decide what would be the BEST order to put sentences to form a well-organized paragraph. Each sentence has a place in the paragraph; there are no extra sentences. *PRINT THE LETTER OF THE CORRECT ANSWER IN THE SPACE AT THE RIGHT.*

Questions 1-3.

DIRECTIONS: Questions 1 through 3 are to be answered on the basis of the following paragraph.

The CDC estimates that food-borne pathogens cause approximately 48 million illnesses, 3,000 deaths, and 128,000 hospitalizations in the United States each year. Contamination with disease-causing microbes called pathogens is usually due to improper food handling or storage. Other causes of food-borne diseases are toxic chemicals or other harmful substances in food and beverages. Food-borne diseases are illnesses caused when people consume contaminated food or beverages. More than 250 food-borne illnesses have been described, according to the United States Centers for Disease Control and Prevention (CDC).

1. When the five sentences are arranged in proper order, the paragraph starts with the sentence that begins:
   A. "Food-borne diseases..."
   B. "More than 250..."
   C. "Other causes of..."
   D. "The CDC estimates..."

1.____

2. If the above paragraph were correctly organized, which of the following transition words would be appropriate to place at the beginning of the sentence that starts "The CDC estimates..."?
   A. With that said
   B. However
   C. To start off
   D. Ultimately

2.____

3. When the above paragraph is properly arranged, it ends with the words:
   A. "...Disease Control and Prevention (CDC).
   B. "...improper food handling or storage."
   C. "...United States each year."
   D. "...in food and beverages."

3.____

Questions 4-7.

DIRECTIONS: Questions 4 through 7 are to be answered on the basis of the following passage.

85

Her father, Abraham Quintanilla, who worked in the shipping department of a chemical plant and later opened a restaurant, had fronted a moderately successful band called Los Dinos ("The Guys") as a young man. Among them, her murder evoked an outpouring of grief comparable to that experienced by other Americans after the deaths of such major cultural figures as President John F. Kennedy. Selena had become an icon in the Hispanic community.

Selena Quintanilla was born in Lake Jackson, Texas, near Houston, on April 16, 1971. She had turned into a beloved figure to whom Mexican-Americans attached their aspirations and their feelings about their cultural identities. The violent death of beloved Tejano vocalist Selena on Mach 31, 1995 brought to an end more than just a promising musical career.

4. When arranged properly, the paragraph's opening sentence should start with: 4.____
   A. "Among them…" B. "The violent death…"
   C. "Her father, Abraham…" D. "Selena had become…"

5. In the second sentence listed above, "them" refers to 5.____
   A. Selena and her fans B. other non-Mexican Americans
   C. Selena and John F. Kennedy D. Mexican-Americans

6. After correctly organizing the paragraph, the author decides to split it into two separate paragraphs. Which of the following would begin the newly made second paragraph? 6.____
   A. "Selena had become…" B. "Selena Quintanilla was…"
   C. "The violent death…" D. "Her father, Abraham…"

7. When correctly organized, the final sentence of the paragraph should end end with the words: 7.____
   A. "…as a young man." B. "…on April 16, 1971."
   C. "…in the Hispanic community." D. "…a promising music career."

Questions 8-10.

DIRECTIONS: Questions 8 through 10 are to be answered on the basis of the following paragraph.

Whether Death takes the form of a decrepit old man, a grim reaper, or a ferryman, his visit is almost never welcome by the poor mortal who finds him at the door. Such is not the case in "Because I Could Not Stop for Death." Knowing that the woman has been keeping herself too busy in her daily life to remember Death, he "kindly" comes by to get her. Perhaps Dickinson's most famous work, "Because I Could Not Stop for Death" is generally considered to be one of the great masterpieces of American poetry. Here, Death is a gentleman, perhaps handsome and well-groomed, who makes a call at the home of a naïve young woman. The poem begins with a comment upon Death's politeness, although he surprises the woman with his visit. While most people would try to bar the door once they recognized his identity, this woman gives the impression that she is quite flattered to find herself in even this gentleman's favor. Death is personified, or described in terms of human characteristics, throughout literature. Figuratively speaking, this poem is about one woman's "date with death." Dickinson uses the personification of Death as a metaphor throughout the poem.

8. Which of the following sentence beginnings indicate the opening sentence of this paragraph?
   A. "Perhaps Dickinson's most..."
   B. "The poem begins with..."
   C. "Death is personified..."
   D. "Whether Death takes..."

   8.____

9. To whom does "his" refer to in the sentence that starts "While most people would..."?
   A. A gentleman
   B. Death
   C. People trying to avoid death
   D. Ms. Dickinson

   9.____

10. If the paragraph were correctly organized, the second to last sentence would end with:
    A. "...gentleman's favor."
    B. "...a naive young woman."
    C. "...of American poetry."
    D. "...throughout literature."

    10.____

Questions 11-13.

DIRECTIONS: Questions 11 through 13 are to be answered on the basis of the following paragraph.

Reformers such as Jacob Riis, author of *The Children of the Tenements* (1903), and George Creel, who with the assistance of Denver's juvenile court judge, Ben Lindsey, wrote *Children in Bondage* (1913), helped broaden awareness of the conditions under which many of the nation's poor children were reared. At the same time, changes were taking place in the way the childhood years were perceived. More and more Americans began to regard children as a national resource that deserved society's protection and guidance. In sharp contrast to these images of child workers worn down by the toil of their labor were the children of the middle class, who led quite different lives and whose progress was measured not in industrial output, but in ways increasingly seen as being vital to their development as productive citizens. Exhibitions of photographs of children employed in all sorts of economic pursuits, including those considered among the most dangerous and grueling, proved equally successful in pricking the public's conscience. When the United States was a nation of farms, shops, and small mills, the use of children to supplement a family's income was so common that it attracted little notice and even less concern. The nation's rapid and dramatic transformation into an industrialized society, however, changed the environment in which children labored and the conditions to which they were exposed.

11. When organized correctly, the third sentence in the above paragraph would start:
    A. "The nation's rapid..."
    B. "In sharp contrast..."
    C. "At the same time..."
    D. "Exhibitions of photographs..."

    11.____

12. If the author wanted to change the beginning of the topic sentence for this paragraph to "In the past," they would need to change which of the following?
    A. "Reformers such as..."
    B. "Exhibitions of photographs..."
    C. "More and more Americans..."
    D. "When the United States..."

    12.____

13. If the above paragraph was organized correctly, its ending words of the last sentence would be:

    13.____

A. "...as productive citizens."
B. "...and even less concern."
C. "...in pricking the public's conscience."
D. "...poor children were reared."

Questions 14-16.

DIRECTIONS: Questions 14 through 16 are to be answered on the basis of the following paragraph.

Here we outline a unique bivariate flood hazard assessment framework that accounts for the interactions between a primary oceanic flooding hazard, coastal water level, and fluvial flooding hazards. Common flood hazard assessment practices typically focus on one flood driver at a time and ignore potential compounding impacts. The results show that, in a warming climate, future sea level rise not only increases the failure probability, but also exacerbates the compounding effects of flood drivers. Using the notion of "failure probability," we also assess coastal flood hazard under different future sea level rise scenarios. Population and assets in coastal regions are threatened by both oceanic and fluvial flooding hazards.

14. When the sentences above are organized correctly, the paragraph starts with the sentence that begins:
    A. "The results show..."
    B. "Here we outline..."
    C. "Population and assets..."
    D. "Using the notion..."

15. If the author wanted to add the phrase "To sum up" to the above paragraph, he would insert it in front of the sentence that begins:
    A. "Using the notion..."
    B. "Common flood hazard..."
    C. "Here we outline..."
    D. "The results show..."

16. Assuming the paragraph were organized correctly, the second to last sentence would end:
    A. "...of flood drivers."
    B. "...level rise scenarios."
    C. "...fluvial flooding hazards."
    D. "...compounding impacts."

Questions 17-19.

DIRECTIONS: Questions 17 through 19 are to be answered on the basis of the following paragraph.

The adhesive stuck to a pig heart even when the surface was coated in blood, the team reported in the July 28 Science. Li, who did the research while at Harvard University, and colleagues also tested the glue in live rats with liver lacerations. A solution might be found under wet leaves on a forest floor, recent research suggests. For surgeons closing internal incisions, that's more than an annoyance. The right glue could hold wounds together as effectively as stitches and staples with less damage to the surrounding soft tissue, enabling safer surgical procedures. It stopped the rats' bleeding, and the animals didn't appear to suffer any bad reaction from the adhesive. Finding a great glue is a sticky task — especially if you want to attach to something as slick as the inside of the human body. Jianyu Li of McGill University in Montreal and colleagues have created a surgical glue that mimics the chemical recipe of goopy slime that slugs exude when they're startled. Using the glue to plug a hole in the pig heart worked so well that the heart still held in liquid after being inflated and deflated tens of thousands of times. Even the strongest human-made adhesives don't work well on wet surfaces like tissues and organs.

17. The above paragraph, when organized correctly, should begin with the words: 17._____
    A. "Finding a great..."   B. "Using the glue..."
    C. "The adhesive stuck..."   D. "It stopped the rats..."

18. If the author wanted to split the paragraph into two separate paragraphs, the 18._____
    first sentence of the second paragraph would begin:
    A. "For surgeons closing..."   B. "Even the strongest..."
    C. "A solution might be..."   D. "Jianyu Li of McGill..."

19. If the above paragraph were organized correctly, the final sentence would 19._____
    end with:
    A. "...recent research suggests."   B. "...from the adhesive."
    C. "...like tissues and organs."   D. "...thousands of times."

Questions 20-22.

DIRECTIONS: Questions 20 to 22 are to be answered on the basis of the following paragraph.

The signal from the spacecraft is gone, and within the next 45 seconds, so will be the spacecraft," Cassini project manager Earl Maize announced from the mission control center at NASA's Jet Propulsion Lab. The signal that Cassini had reached its destination arrived at Earth at 4:54 A.M., and cut out about a minute later as the spacecraft lost its battle with Saturn's atmosphere. I'm going to call this the end of mission. Project manager, off the net." With that, the mission control team erupted in applause, hugs and some tears. This has been an incredible mission, an incredible spacecraft, and you're all an incredible team. The spacecraft entered Saturn's atmosphere at about 3:31 A.M. PDT on September 15 and immediately began running through all of its stabilizing procedures to try to keep itself upright. Cassini went down fighting. After 20 years in space and 13 years orbiting Saturn, the veteran spacecraft spent its last 90 seconds or so firing its thrusters as hard as it could to keep sending Saturnian secrets back to Earth for as long as possible.

20. In the above paragraph, who does "you all" refer to in the sentence that begins 20._____
    "Congratulations"?
    A. All Americans   B. Cassini
    C. Earl Maize   D. The mission control team

21. If the sentence were organized correctly, the fourth sentence's last words 21._____
    would be:
    A. "...as long as possible."   B. "...this amazing accomplishment."
    C. "...Saturn's atmosphere."   D. "...off the net."

22. When organized correctly, the final sentence would end with the following: 22._____
    A. "...and some tears."   B. "...went down fighting."
    C. "...Jet Propulsion Lab."   D. "...keep itself upright."

Questions 23-25.

DIRECTIONS: Questions 23 through 25 are to be answered on the basis of the following paragraph.

As the first African-American woman to carry mail, she stood out on the trail — and became a Wild West legend. Born Mary Fields in around 1832, Fields was born into slavery, and like many other enslaved people, her exact date of birth is not known. Rumor had it that she'd fending off an angry pack of wolves with her rifle, had "the temperament of a grizzly bear," and was not above a gunfight. Bandits beware: In 1890s Montana, would-be mail thieves didn't stand a chance against Stagecoach Mary. Even the place of her birth is questionable, though historians have pinpointed Hickman County, Tennessee as the most likely location. At the time, slaves were treated like pieces of property; their numbers were recorded in record books, their names were not. But how much of Stagecoach Mary's story is myth? The hard-drinking, quick-shooting mail carrier sported two guns, men's clothing, and a bad attitude.

23. Who does "she'd" refer to in the sentence that begins "Rumor had it..."? 23.____
    A. An anonymous African-American   B. Hickman County
    C. A mail thief   D. Stagecoach Mary

24. If the author were interested in splitting this paragraph into two separate paragraphs, the topic sentence of the second paragraph would begin: 24.____
    A. "At the time..."   B. "Born Mary Fields..."
    C. "Bandits beware..."   D. "As the first..."

25. When organized correctly, the final sentence of the paragraph would end with the words: 25.____
    A. "...their names were not."   B. "...above a gunfight."
    C. "...against Stagecoach Mary."   D. "...a Wild West legend."

KEY (CORRECT ANSWERS)

1. A
2. D
3. C
4. B
5. D

6. B
7. A
8. C
9. B
10. A

11. C
12. D
13. A
14. C
15. D

16. B
17. A
18. C
19. B
20. D

21. C
22. A
23. D
24. B
25. A

TEST 2

DIRECTIONS: Each question or incomplete statement is followed by several suggested answers or completions. Select the one that BEST answers the question or completes the statement. *PRINT THE LETTER OF THE CORRECT ANSWER IN THE SPACE AT THE RIGHT.*

Questions 1-3.

DIRECTIONS: Questions 1 through 3 are to be answered on the basis of the following paragraph.

The majority of people who develop these issues are athletes who participate in popular high-impact sports, especially football. Although most people who suffer a concussion experience initial bouts of dizziness, nausea, and drowsiness, these symptoms often disappear after a few days. Although both new sports regulations and improvements in helmet technology can help protect players, the sports media and fans alike bear some of the responsibility for reducing the incidence of these devastating injuries. These psychological problems can include depression, anxiety, memory loss, inability to concentrate, and aggression. In extreme cases, people suffering from CTE have even committed suicide or homicide. The long-term effects of concussions, however, are less understood and far more severe. Recent studies suggest that people who suffer multiple concussions are at a significant risk for developing chronic traumatic encephalopathy (CTE), a degenerative brain disorder that causes a variety of dangerous mental and emotional problems to arise weeks, months, or even years after the initial injury. Chronic Traumatic Encephalopathy Concussions are brain injuries that occur when a person receives a blow to the head, face, or neck.

1. When organized correctly, the first sentence of the paragraph begins with: 1._____
   A. "Recent studies suggest..." B. "The long-term effects..."
   C. "Although both new..." D. "Chronic Traumatic..."

2. Upon ordering the paragraph correctly, the author wishes to substitute for a word in sentence four that means "progressive irreversible deterioration." Which word does the author wish to replace? 2._____
   A. Anxiety B. Degenerative
   C. Responsibility D. Devastating

3. If put in the right order, the paragraph's last words would be: 3._____
   A. "...to the head, face, or neck."
   B. "...committed suicide or homicide."
   C. "...these devastating injuries."
   D. "...far more severe."

Questions 4-8.

DIRECTIONS: Questions 4 through 8 are to be answered on the basis of the following paragraph.

These controversies were settled by the 1977 treaty, which provided for a twenty-two-year period of U.S. withdrawal and turnover of the canal to Panama. For its first 85 years the canal was operate exclusively by the United States government as an international maritime passage, according to the 1903 Hay-Buneau-Varilla Treaty and the 1977 Carter-Torrijos Treaty that replaced it. Panamanian and other critics pointed out that the United States took unfair advantage of the newly independent republic (separated from Colombia in 1903, with the help of the United States) to impose conditions for near-sovereign ownership; complained that it exceeded its original concession by creating a strategic military complex with fourteen bases and numerous intelligence sites; and asserted that it created a virtual state within a state by establishing public agencies and enterprises in the 500-plus square miles of territory it controlled in the Canal Zone. One of the world's great engineering projects, the canal was controversial because of the method by which the United States gained the concession (by negotiating a treaty with a French shareholder temporarily representing Panama) and its operation of the utility with regard to the interests of Panama. Built between 1904 and 1914, the canal shortened maritime voyages considerably. The Panama Canal is a 51-mile ship canal with six pairs of locks that crosses the Isthmus of Panama and allows vessels to transit between the Caribbean Sea and the Pacific Ocean. Under the latter treaty, the canal was turned over in 1999 to the Republic of Panama, which has operated it ever since.

4. When organized correctly, the sentence AFTERs the topic sentence should begin:
   A. "Built between 1904..."
   B. "The Panama Canal..."
   C. "These controversies..."
   D. "Panamanian and other..."

5. If the author ordered the sentences correctly, one sentence that provides evidence of controversy surrounding the Panama Canal would be Sentence
   A. 7   B. 5   C. 1   D. 2

6. When correctly ordered, the last words of the paragraph would be:
   A. "...the canal to Panama."
   B. "...in the Canal Zone."
   C. "...and the Pacific Ocean."
   D. "...to the interests of Panama."

7. What "latter treaty" is the sentence that begins "Under the latter treaty..." referring to in the paragraph?
   A. The Treaty of Panama
   B. The Hay-Buneau-Varilla Treaty
   C. The Carter-Torrijos Treaty
   D. Both B and C

8. When organized correctly, the sentence that ends "...in the Canal Zone" would be preceded by the sentence that begins:
   A. "The Panama Canal..."
   B. "These controversies were..."
   C. "For its first..."
   D. "One of the world's great..."

Questions 9-11.

DIRECTIONS: Questions 9 through 11 are to be answered on the basis of the following paragraph.

Such incidents revolved around many issues, including, among others, job security, wages, occupational safety, and, especially, the eight-hour day. The Haymarket Riot of 1886 grew out of a long string of circumstances that eventually culminated in an unfortunate incident. Not only were skilled craftsmen seeing their professions disappear in the face of machines operated by unskilled labor, but the length of hours in the workday lengthened and could range from ten to twelve and even longer in some specific instances. It was this last issue that was particularly important as the Industrial Revolution truly swept over America. Regardless of who might have been at fault in a labor struggle, each moment of violent upheaval had serious consequences. During the post-Civil War era, there were periods of labor upheaval both in Chicago and across the nation. Each of these topics played an important role in labor unrest as the climate in the country between workers and the state reached fever pitch. At issue were several key points: the continued growth of the Industrial Revolution and its impact on society, the movement for the eight-hour workday, worker dissatisfaction, suppression of labor activities by various government authorities, and the growth of radicalism in the United States.

9. If the author were to put the paragraph in the correct order, the third sentence would begin with the words:
   A. "Each of these…"
   B. "It was this last…"
   C. "Not only were skilled…"
   D. "The Haymarket Riot…"

10. The author has determined that one paragraph is too long, so they wish to split it into two paragraphs and change the start of the new paragraph to "Dating back to". The sentence that the author would need to alter slightly currently begins:
    A. "The Haymarket Riot…"
    B. "Each of these topics…"
    C. "During the post-Civil…"
    D. "Not only were…"

11. When organized correctly, the last sentence of the paragraph would end with the words:
    A. "…an unfortunate incident."
    B. "…some specific instances."
    C. "…in the United States."
    D. "…across the nation."

Questions 12-14.

DIRECTIONS: Questions 12 through 14 are to be answered on the basis of the following paragraph.

Using an experimental design, they find no evidence that the use of Twitter improves students' learning. The authors assess students across three different institutions to see if the use of Twitter improves learning outcomes relative to a traditional Learning Management System. Ever since Becker and Watts (1996) found that economic educators rely heavily on "chalk and talk" as a primary teaching method, economic educators have been seeking new ways to engage students and improve learning outcomes. Recently, the use of social media as a pedagogical tool in economics has received increasing interest.

12. When organized correctly, the paragraph would begin with the words:
    A. "Using an..."
    B. "Recently, the..."
    C. "The authors..."
    D. "Ever since..."

13. In the sentence that begins "Using an experimental...", to whom does "they" refer?
    A. Social media users
    B. Becker and Watts
    C. Economic educators
    D. Different institutions

14. If the author wanted to start the last sentence with "With that said...", they would be adding it to the sentence that currently starts:
    A. "Using an..."
    B. "The authors..."
    C. "Recently, the..."
    D. "Ever since..."

Questions 15-17.

DIRECTIONS: Questions 15 through 17 are to be answered on the basis of the following paragraph.

Teaching the topic of genetics in relationship to ancestry and race generates many questions, and requires a teaching strategy that encourages perspective-based exploration and discussion. We have developed a set of dialogues for discussing the complex science of genetics, ancestry, and race that is contextualized in real human interactions and that contends with the social and ethical implications of this science. This article provides some brief historical and scientific context for these dialogues, describes their development, and relates how we have used them in different ways to engage diverse groups of science learners. The dialogue series can be incorporated into classroom or informal science education settings. After listening to or performing the dialogues and participating in a discussion, students will: (1) recognize misunderstandings about the relationship between DNA and race; (2) describe how DNA testing services assign geographic ancestry; (3) explain how scientific findings have been used historically to promote institutionalized racism and the role personal biases can play in science; (4) identify situations in their own life that have affected their understanding of genetics and race; and (5) discuss the potential consequences of the racialization of medicine as well as other fallacies about the connection of science and race.

15. If the author organized the above paragraph correctly, the fourth sentence would end with the words:
    A. "...connection of science and race."
    B. "...implications of this science."
    C. "...exploration and discussion."
    D. "...science education settings."

16. The author wishes to split the paragraph into two distinct paragraphs. When organized, the last sentence of the first paragraph would begin:
    A. "We have developed..."
    B. "This article proves..."
    C. "The dialogue series..."
    D. "Teaching the topic..."

17. When organized correctly, the last sentence would begin with the words: 17.____
   A. "After listening to..."   B. "Teaching the topic..."
   C. "We have developed..."   D. "This article provides..."

Questions 18-20.

DIRECTIONS: Questions 18 through 20 are to be answered on the basis of the following paragraph.

For example, Canadian Immigration officers have the power to deny persons with OWI convictions from crossing the border into Canada. Individuals who have been acquitted of an OWI can still be stopped at the border and denied entry. Some restrictions, however, are not known to individuals that have been charged with an OWI. In fact, if you have been arrested or convicted for driving under the influence of drugs or alcohol, regardless of whether it was a felony or a misdemeanor, you may be criminally inadmissible to Canada or denied entry. In order to receive an eTA, individuals have to disclose their criminal convictions, which may bar them from entering Canada. The restrictions imposed by an OWI conviction can be quite burdensome. Even if you will not be driving in Canada, you can still be denied entry. This stringent border patrol comes as a surprise to many U.S. citizens. Canadian Immigration Officials have introduced a new entry requirement, known as an Electronic Travel Authorization (eTA).

18. When organized correctly, the topic sentence of the paragraph would begin with the words: 18.____
   A. "This stringent border..."   B. "In fact, if..."
   C. "Canadian Immigration Officials..."   D. "The restrictions imposed..."

19. Once properly ordered, it would make the most sense to insert the words "With that being the case..." in front of the sentence that currently begins: 19.____
   A. "The restrictions imposed..."   B. "For example..."
   C. "Canadian Immigration Officials..."   D. "Even if you will..."

20. If the author were to put the paragraph in correct order, the second to last sentence would end with the words: 20.____
   A. "...border into Canada."   B. "...from entering Canada."
   C. "...to many U.S. citizens."   D. "...to Canada or denied entry."

Questions 21-25.

DIRECTIONS: Questions 21 through 25 are to be answered on the basis of the following paragraph.

Many instructors at the college level require that you use scholarly articles as sources when writing a research paper. Scholarly or peer-reviewed articles are written by experts in academic or professional fields. They are excellent sources for finding out what has been studied or researched on a topic as well as to find bibliographies that point to other relevant sources of information. Peer-reviewed journals require that articles are read and evaluated by experts in the field before they are accepted for publication. Although most scholarly articles are refereed or peer reviewed, some are not. Generally, instructors are happy with either peer-reviewed or scholarly articles, but if your article HAS to be peer-reviewed, you will need to find that information in the front of the journal, or use Ulrich's Periodicals Directory (Reference Z6941 U5) located behind the Reference Desk on the 2nd floor of the library. Look up your title and look for the Document Type: Journal, Academic/Scholarly. Articles that are peer-reviewed will have an arrow to the left of the title.

21. When organized correctly, the introductory sentence would begin with the words: 21.____
    A. "They are excellent…"   B. "Peer-reviewed journals…"
    C. "Many instructors at…"   D. "Look up your…"

22. In the sentence that begins "They are", to what/whom does "They" refer? 22.____
    A. Scholarly articles   B. Instructors
    C. Peers   D. Library directory

23. If the author were interested in splitting up the paragraph into two separate paragraphs, the topic sentence of the second paragraph would begin: 23.____
    A. "Many instructors at…"   B. "Peer-reviewed journals…"
    C. "Generally instructors are…"   D. "Scholarly or peer-reviewed…"

24. When organized correctly, the third sentence of the paragraph would end with the words: 24.____
    A. "…a research paper."   B. "…of the title."
    C. "…of the library."   D. "…sources of information."

25. If the author were to organize the paragraph correctly, the paragraph would end with the words: 25.____
    A. "…some are not."   B. "…a research paper."
    C. "…or professional fields."   D. "…of the title."

KEY (CORRECT ANSWERS)

1.	D		11.	B
2.	B		12.	D
3.	C		13.	B
4.	A		14.	A
5.	B		15.	D
6.	A		16.	C
7.	C		17.	A
8.	D		18.	D
9.	A		19.	C
10.	C		20.	B

21. C
22. A
23. B
24. D
25. D

EXAMINATION SECTION
TEST 1

DIRECTIONS: The sentences listed below are part of a meaningful paragraph, but they are not given in their proper order. You are to decide what would be the BEST order to put sentences to form a well-organized paragraph. Each sentence has a place in the paragraph; there are no extra sentences. *PRINT THE LETTER OF THE CORRECT ANSWER IN THE SPACE AT THE RIGHT.*

1.
   I. He came on a winter's eve.
   II. Akira came directly, breaking all tradition.
   III. He pounded on the door while a cold rain beat on the shuttered veranda, so at first Chie thought him only the wind.
   IV. Was that it?
   V. Had he followed form—had he asked his mother to speak to his father to approach a go-between—would Chie have been more receptive?
   The CORRECT answer is:
   A. II, IV, V, I, III   B. I, III, II, IV, V   C. V, IV, II, III, I   D. III, V, I, II, IV

   1.____

2.
   I. We have an understanding.
   II. Either method comes down to the same thing: a matter of parental approval.
   III. If you give your consent, I become Naomi's husband.
   IV. Please don't judge my candidacy by the unseemliness of this proposal.
   V. I ask directly because the use of a go-between takes much time.
   The CORRECT answer is:
   A. III, IV, II, V, I   B. I, V, II, III, IV   C. I, IV, V, II, III   D. V, III, I, IV, II

   2.____

3.
   I. Many relish the opportunity to buy presents because gift-giving offers a powerful means to build stronger bonds with one's closest peers.
   II. Aside from purchasing holiday gifts, most people regularly buy presents for other occasions throughout the year, including weddings, birthdays, anniversaries, graduations, and baby showers.
   III. Last year, Americans spent over $30 billion at retail stores in the month of December alone.
   IV. This frequent experience of gift-giving can engender ambivalent feelings in gift-givers.
   V. Every day, millions of shoppers hit the stores in full force—both online and on foot—searching frantically for the perfect gift.
   The CORRECT answer is:
   A. II, III, V, I, IV   B. IV, V, I, III, II   C. III, II, V, I, IV   D. V, III, II, IV, I

   3.____

4. I. Why do gift-givers assume that gift price is closely linked to gift-recipients' feelings of appreciation?
    II. Perhaps givers believe that bigger (i.e., more expensive) gifts convey stronger signals of thoughtfulness and consideration.
    III. In this sense, gift-givers may be motivated to spend more money on a gift in order to send a "stronger signal" to their intended recipient.
    IV. According to Camerer (1988) and others, gift-giving represents a symbolic ritual, whereby gift-givers attempt to signal their positive attitudes toward the intended recipient and their willingness to invest resources in a future relationship.
    V. As for gift-recipients, they may not construe smaller and larger gifts as representing smaller and larger signals of thoughtfulness and consideration.
    The CORRECT answer is:
    A. V, III, II, IV, I   B. I, II, IV, III, V   C. IV, I, III, V, II   D. II, V, I, IV, III

5. I. But when the spider is not hungry, the stimulation of its hairs merely causes it to shake the touched limb.
    II. Touching this body hair produces one of two distinct reactions.
    III. The entire body of a tarantula, especially its legs, is thickly clothed with hair.
    IV. Some of it is short and wooly, some long and stiff.
    V. When the spider is hungry, it responds with an immediate and swift attack.
    The CORRECT answer is:
    A. IV, II, I, III, V   B. V, I, III, IV, II   C. III, IV, II, V, I   D. I, II, IV, III, V

6. I. That tough question may be just one question away from an easy one.
    II. They tend to be arranged sequentially: questions on the first paragraph come before questions on the second paragraph.
    III. In summation, it is important not to forget that there is no penalty for guessing.
    IV. Try *all* questions on the passage.
    V. Remember, the critical reading questions after each passage are not arranged in order of difficulty.
    The CORRECT answer is:
    A. I, III, IV, II, V   B. II, I, V, III, IV   C. III, IV, I, V, II   D. V, II, IV, I, III

7. I. This time of year clients come to me with one goal in mind: losing weight.
    II. I usually tell them that their goal should be focused on fat loss instead of weight loss.
    III. Converting and burning fat while maintaining or building muscle is an art, which also happens to be my job.
    IV. What I love about this line of work is that *everyone* benefits from healthy eating and supplemental nutrition.
    V. This is because most of us have more stored fat than we prefer, but we do not want to lose muscle in addition to the fat.
    The CORRECT answer is:
    A. V, III, I, II, IV   B. I, IV, V, III, IV   C. II, I, III, IV, V   D. II, V, IV, I, II

8. I. In Tierra del Fuego, "invasive" describes the beaver perfectly.
    II. What started as a small influx of 50 beavers has since grown to a number over 200,000.
    III. Unlike in North America where the beaver has several natural predators that help to maintain manageable population numbers, Tierra del Fuego has no such luxury.
    IV. An invasive species is a non-indigenous animal, fungus, or plant species introduced to an area that has the potential to inflict harm upon the native ecosystem.
    V. It was first introduced in 1946 by the Argentine government in an effort to catalyze a fur trading industry in the region.
    The CORRECT answer is:
    A. IV, I, V, II, III   B. I, IV, II, III, V   C. II, V, III, I, IV   D. V, II, IV, III, I

9. I. The words ensure that we are all part of something much larger than the here and now.
    II. Literature might be thought of as the creative measure of history.
    III. It seems impossible to disconnect most literary works from their historical context.
    IV. Great writers, poets, and playwrights mold their sense of life and the events of their time into works of art.
    V. However, the themes that make their work universal and enduring perhaps do transcend time.
    The CORRECT answer is:
    A. I, III, II, V, IV   B. IV, I, V, II, III   C. II, IV, III, V, I   D. III, V, I, IV, II

10. I. If you don't already have an exercise routine, try to build up to a good 20- to 45-minute aerobic workout.
    II. When your brain is well oxygenated, it works more efficiently, so you do your work better and faster.
    III. Your routine will help you enormously when you sit down to work on homework or even on the day of a test.
    IV. Twenty minutes of cardiovascular exercise is a great warm-up before you start your homework.
    V. Exercise does not just help your muscles; it also helps your brain.
    The CORRECT answer is:
    A. I, IV, II, IV, III   B. IV, V, II, I, III   C. V, III, IV, II, I   D. III, IV, I, V, II

11. I. Experts often suggest that crime resembles an epidemic, but what kind?
    II. If it travels along major transportation routes, the cause is microbial.
    III. Economics professor Karl Smith has a good rule of thumb for categorizing epidemics: if it is along the lines of communication, he says the cause is information.
    IV. However, if it spreads everywhere all at once, the cause is a molecule.
    V. If it spreads out like a fan, the cause is an insect.
    The CORRECT answer is:
    A. I, III, II, V, IV   B. II, I, V, IV, III   C. V, III, I, II, IV   D. IV, V, I, III, II

12.
   I. A recent study had also suggested a link between childhood lead exposure and juvenile delinquency later on.
   II. These ideas all caused Nevin to look into other sources of lead-based items as well, such as gasoline.
   III. In 1994, Rick Nevin was a consultant working for the U.S Department of Housing and Urban Development on the costs and benefits of removing lead paint from old houses.
   IV. Maybe reducing lead exposure could have an effect on violent crime too?
   V. A growing body of research had linked lead exposure in small children with a whole raft of complications later in life, including lower IQ and behavioral problems.
   The CORRECT answer is:
   A. I, III, V, II, IV   B. IV, I, II, V, III   C. I, III, V, IV, II   D. III, V, I, IV, II

13.
   I. Like Lord Byron a century earlier, he had learn to play himself, his own best hero, with superb conviction.
   II. Or maybe he was Tarzan Hemingway, crouching in the African bush with elephant gun at the ready.
   III. He was Hemingway of the rugged outdoor grin and the hairy chest posing beside the lion he had just shot.
   IV. But even without the legend, the chest-beating, wisecracking pose that was later to seem so absurd, his impact upon us was tremendous.
   V. By the time we were old enough to read Hemingway, he had become legendary.
   The CORRECT answer is:
   A. I, V, II, IV, III   B. II, I, III, IV, V   C. IV, II, V, III, I   D. V, I, III, II, IV

14.
   I. Why do the electrons that inhabit atoms jump around so strangely, from one bizarrely shaped orbital to another?
   II. And most importantly, why do protons, the bits that give atoms their heft and personality, stick together at all?
   III. Why are some atoms, like sodium, so hyperactive while others, like helium, are so aloof?
   IV. As any good contractor will tell you, a sound structure requires stable materials.
   V. But atoms, the building blocks of everything we know and love—brownies and butterflies and beyond—do not appear to be models of stability.
   The CORRECT answer is:
   A. IV, V, III, I, II   B. V, III, I, II, IV   C. I, IV, II, V, III   D. III, I, IV, II, V

15.
   I. Current atomic theory suggests that the strong nuclear force is most likely conveyed by massless particles called "gluons".
   II. According to quantum chromodynamics (QCD), protons and neutrons are composed of smaller particles called quarks, which are held together by the gluons.
   III. As a quantum theory, it conceives of space and time as tiny chunks that occasionally misbehave, rather than smooth predictable quantities.

IV. If you are hoping that QCD ties up atomic behavior with a tidy little bow, you will be disappointed.
V. This quark-binding force has "residue" that extends beyond protons and neutrons themselves to provide enough force to bind the protons and neutrons together.

The CORRECT answer is:
A. III, IV, II, V, I   B. II, I, IV, III, V   C. I, II, V, IV, III   D. V, III, I, IV, II

16.
I. I have seen him whip a woman, causing the blood to run half an hour at a time.
II. Mr. Severe, the overseer, used to stand by the door of the quarter, armed with a large hickory stick, ready to whip anyone who was not ready to start at the sound of the horn.
III. This was in the midst of her crying children, pleading for their mother's release.
IV. He seemed to take pleasure in manifesting his fiendish barbarity.
V. Mr. Severe was rightly named: he was a cruel man.

The CORRECT answer is:
A. I, IV, III, II, I   B. II, V, I, III, IV   C. II, V, III, I, IV   D. IV, III, I, V, II

17.
I. His death was recorded by the slaves as the result of a merciful providence.
II. His career was cut short.
III. He died very soon after I went to Colonel Lloyd's; and he died as he lived, uttering bitter curses and horrid oaths.
IV. Mr. Severe's place was filled by a Mr. Hopkins.
V. From the rising till the going down of the sun, he was cursing, raving, cutting, and slashing among the slaves in the field.

The CORRECT answer is:
A. V, II, III, I, IV   B. IV, I, III, II, V   C. III, I, IV, V, II   D. I, II, V, III, IV

18.
I. The primary reef-building organisms are invertebrate animals known as corals.
II. They are located in warm, shallow, tropical marine waters with enough light to stimulate the growth of reef organisms.
III. Coral reefs are highly diverse ecosystems, supporting greater numbers of fish species than any other marine ecosystem.
IV. They belong to the class Anthozoa and are subdivided into stony corals, which have six tentacles.
V. These corals are small colonial, marine invertebrates.

The CORRECT answer is:
A. I, IV, V, II, III   B. V, I, III, IV, II   C. III, II, I, V, IV   D. IV, V, II, III, I

19.
I. Jane Goodall, an English ethologist, is famous for her studies of the chimpanzees of the Gombe Stream Reserve in Tanzania.
II. As a result of her studies, Goodall concluded that chimpanzees are an advanced species closely related to humans.
III. Ultimately, Goodall's observations led her to write *The Chimpanzee Family Book*, which conveys a new, more humane view of wildlife.

IV. She is credited with the first recorded observation of chimps eating meat and using and making tools.
V. Her observations have forced scientists to redefine the characteristics once considered as solely human traits.
The CORRECT answer is:
A. V, II, IV, III, I   B. I, IV, II, V, III   C. I, II, V, IV, III   D. III, V, II, I, IV

20. I. Since then, research has demonstrated that the deposition of atmospheric chemicals is causing widespread acidification of lakes, streams, and soil.
II. "Acid rain" is a popularly used phrase that refers to the deposition of acidifying substances from the atmosphere.
III. This phenomenon became a prominent issue around 1970.
IV. Of the many chemicals that are deposited from the atmosphere, the most important in terms of causing acidity in soil and surface waters are dilute solutions of sulfuric and nitric acids.
V. These chemicals are deposited as acidic rain or snow and include sulfur dioxide, oxides of nitrogen, and tiny particulates such as ammonium sulfate.
The CORRECT answer is:
A. III, IV, I, II, V   B. IV, III, I, IV, V   C. V, I, IV, III, II   D. II, III, I, IV, V

21. I. Programmers wrote algorithmic software that precisely specified both the problem and how to solve it.
II. AI programmers, in contrast, have sought to program computers with flexible rules for seeking solutions to problems.
III. In the 1940 and 1950s, the first large, electronic, digital computers were designed to perform numerical calculations set up by a human programmer.
IV. The computers did so by completing a series of clearly defined steps, or algorithms.
V. An AI program may be designed to modify the rules it is given or to develop entirely new rules.
The CORRECT answer is:
A. I, III, II, V, IV   B. IV, I, III, V, II   C. III, IV, I, II, V   D. III, I, II, IV, V

22. I. Wildfire is a periodic ecological disturbance, associated with the rapid combustion of much of the biomass of an ecosystem.
II. Wildfires themselves are both routine and ecologically necessary.
III. It is where they encounter human habitation, of course, that dangers quickly escalate,
IV. Once ignited by lightning or by humans, the biomass oxidizes as an uncontrolled blaze.
V. This unfettered burning continues until the fire either runs out of fuel or is quenched.
The CORRECT answer is:
A. V, IV, I, II, III   B. I, II, V, III, IV   C. III, II, I, IV, V   D. IV, V, III, I, II

23.
   I. His arguments supported the positions advanced by the Democratic Party's southern wing and sharply challenged the constitutionality of the Republican Party's emerging political platform.
   II. Beginning in the mid-1840s as a simple freedom suit, the case ended with the Court's intervention in the central political issues of the 1850s and the intensification of the sectional crisis that ultimately led to civil war.
   III. During the Civil War, the decision quickly fell into disrepute, and its major rulings were overruled by ratification of the 13th and 14th Amendments.
   IV. *Dred Scott v. Sandford* ranks as one of the worst decisions in the Supreme Court's history.
   V. Chief Justice Roger Taney, speaking for a deeply divided Court, brought about this turn of events by ruling that no black American—whether free or enslaved—could be a U.S. citizen and that Congress possessed no legitimate authority to prohibit slavery's expansion into the federal territories.
   The CORRECT answer is:
   A. II, IV, I, III, V   B. V, I, III, IV, II   C. I, V, II, V, III   D. IV, II, V, I, III

24.
   I. Considered the last battle between the U.S. Army and American Indians, the Wounded Knee Massacre took place on the morning of 29 December 1890 beside Wounded Knee Creek on South Dakota's Pine Ridge Reservation.
   II. This was the culmination of the Ghost Dance religion that had started with a Paiute prophet from Nevada named Wovoka (1856-1932), who was also known as Jack Wilson.
   III. During the previous year, U.S. government officials had reduced Sioux lands and cut back rations so severely that the Sioux people were starving.
   IV. These conditions encouraged the desperate embrace of the Ghost Dance.
   V. This pan-tribal ritual had historical antecedents that go much further back than its actual founder.
   The CORRECT answer is:
   A. I, II, III, IV, V   B. V, IV, II, III, I   C. IV, III, I, V, II   D. III, I, V, II, IV

25.
   I. Their actions, which became known as the Boston Tea Party, set in motion events that led directly to the American Revolution.
   II. Urged on by a crowd of cheering townspeople, the disguised Bostonians destroyed 342 chests of tea estimated to be worth between $10,000 an $18,000.
   III. The Americans, who numbered around 70, shared a common aim: to destroy the ships' cargo of British East India Company tea.
   IV. Many years later, George Hewes, a 31-year-old shoemaker and participant, recalled "We then were ordered by our commander to open the hatches and take out all the chests of tea and throw them overboard. And we immediately proceeded to execute his orders, first cutting and splitting the chests with our tomahawks, so as thoroughly to expose them to the effects of the water.

V. At nine o'clock on the night of December 16, 1773, a band of Bostonians disguised as Native Americans boarded the British merchant ship Dartmouth and two companion vessels anchored at Griffin's Wharf in Boston harbor.

The CORRECT answer is:
A. V, III, IV, II, I   B. IV, II, III, I, V   C. III, IV, V, II, I   D. V, II, IV, III, I

KEY (CORRECT ANSWERS)

1.	A	11.	A
2.	C	12.	D
3.	D	13.	D
4.	B	14.	A
5.	C	15.	C
6.	D	16.	B
7.	B	17.	A
8.	A	18.	C
9.	C	19.	B
10.	B	20.	D

21.	C
22.	B
23.	D
24.	A
25.	A

TEST 2

DIRECTIONS: The sentences listed below are part of a meaningful paragraph, but they are not given in their proper order. You are to decide what would be the BEST order to put sentences to form a well-organized paragraph. Each sentence has a place in the paragraph; there are no extra sentences. *PRINT THE LETTER OF THE CORRECT ANSWER IN THE SPACE AT THE RIGHT.*

1.   I. Recently, some U.S. cities have added a new category: compost, organic matter such as food scraps and yard debris.
    II. For example, paper may go in one container, glass and aluminum in another, regular garbage in a third.
    III. Like paper or glass recycling, compositing demands a certain amount of effort from the public in order to be successful.
    IV. Over the past generation, people in many parts of the United States have become accustomed to dividing their household waste products into different categories for recycling.
    V. But the inconveniences of composting are far outweighed by its benefits.
    The CORRECT answer is:
    A. V, II, III, IV, I   B. I, III, IV, V, II   C. IV, II, I, III, V   D. III, I, V, II, IV

1.____

2.   I. It also enhances soil texture, encouraging healthy roots and minimizing the need for chemical fertilizers.
    II. Most people think of banana peels, eggshells, and dead leaves as "waste," but compost is actually a valuable resource with multiple practical uses.
    III. When utilized as a garden fertilizer, compost provides nutrients to soil and improves plant growth while deterring or killing pests and preventing some plant diseases.
    IV. In large quantities, compost can be converted into a natural gas that can be used as fuel for transportation or heating and cooling systems.
    V. Better than soil at holding moisture, compost minimizes water waste and storm runoff, increases savings on watering costs, and helps reduce erosion on embankments near bodies of water.
    The CORRECT answer is:
    A. II, III, I, V, IV   B. I, IV, V, III, II   C. V, II, IV, I,III   D. III, V, II, IV, I

2.____

3.   I. The street is a sea of red, the traditional Chinese color of luck and happiness.
    II. Buildings are draped with festive, red banners and garlands.
    III. Crowds gather then to celebrate Lunar New Year.
    IV. Lamp posts are strung with crimson paper lanterns, which bob in the crisp winter breeze.
    V. At the beginning of February, thousands of people line H Street, the heart of Chinatown in Washington, D.C.
    The CORRECT answer is:
    A. I, V, II, III, IV   B. IV, II, V, I, III   C. III, I, II, IV, V   D. V, III, I, II, IV

3.____

4. I. Experts agree that the lion dance originated in the Han dynasty; however, there is little agreement about the dance's original purpose.
    II. Another theory is that an emperor, upon waking from a dream about a lion, hired an artist to choreograph the dance.
    III. Dancers must be synchronized with the music accompanying the dance, as well as with each other, in order to fully realize the celebration.
    IV. Whatever the origins are, the current function of the dance is celebration.
    V. Some evidence suggests that the earliest version of the dance was an attempt to ward off an evil spirt.
    The CORRECT answer is:
    A. V, II, IV, III, I   B. I, V, II, IV, III   C. II, I, III, V, IV   D. IV, III, V, I, II

5. I. Half the population of New York, Toronto, and London do not own cars; instead they use public transport.
    II. Every day, subway systems carry 155 million passengers, thirty-four times the number carried by all the world's airplanes.
    III. Though there are 600 million cars on the planet, and counting, there are also seven billion people, which means most of us get around taking other modes of transportation.
    IV. All of that is to say that even a century and a half after the invention of the internal combustion engine, private car ownership is still an anomaly.
    V. In other words, traveling to work, school, or the market means being a straphanger: someone who relies on public transport.
    The CORRECT answer is:
    A. I, II, IV, V, III   B. III, V, I, II, IV   C. III, I, II, IV, V   D. II, IV, V, III, I

6. I. "They jumped up like popcorn," he said, describing how they would flap their half-formed wings and take short hops into the air.
    II. Dan settled on the Chukar Partridge as a model species, but he might not have made his discovery without the help of a local rancher that supplied him with the birds.
    III. At field sites around the world, Dan Kiel saw a pattern in how young ground birds ran along behind their parents.
    IV. So when a group of graduate students challenged him to come up with new data on the age-old ground-up-tree-down debate, he designed a project to see what clues might lie in how baby game birds learned to fly.
    V. When the rancher stopped by to see how things were progressing, he yelled at Dan to give the birds something to climb on.
    The CORRECT answer is:
    A. IV, II, V, I, III   B. III, II, I, V, IV   C. III, I, IV, II, V   D. I, II, IV, V, III

7. I. Honey bees are hosts to the pathogenic large ectoparasitic mite, *Varroa destructor*.
    II. These mites feed on bee hemolymph (blood) and can kill bees directly or by increasing their susceptibility to secondary infections.
    III. Little is known about the natural defenses that keep the mite infections under control.

IV. Pyrethrums are a group of flowering plants that produce potent insecticides with anti-mite activity.
V. In fact, the human mite infestation known as scabies is treated with a topical pyrethrum cream.
The CORRECT answer is:
A. I, II, III, IV, V B. V, IV, II, I, III C. III, IV, V, I, II D. II, IV, I, III, V

8. I. He hardly ever allowed me to pay for the books he placed in my hands, but when he wasn't looking I'd leave the coins I'd managed to collect on the counter.
    II. My favorite place in the whole city was the Sempere & Sons bookshop on Calle Santa Ana.
    III. It smelled of old paper and dust and it was my sanctuary, my refuge.
    IV. The bookseller would let me sit on a chair in a corner and read any book I liked to my heart's content.
    V. It was only small change—if I'd had to buy a book with that pittance, I would probably have been able to afford only a booklet of cigarette papers.
    The CORRECT answer is:
    A. I, III, V, II, IV B. II, IV, I, III, V C. V, I, III, IV, II D. II, III, IV, I, V

9. I. At school, I had learned to read and write long before the other children.
    II. My father, however, did not see things the way I did; he did not like to see books in the house.
    III. Where my school friends saw notches of ink on incomprehensible pages, I saw light, streets, and people.
    IV. Back then my only friends were made of paper and ink.
    V. Words and the mystery of their hidden science fascinated me, and I saw in them a key with which I could unlock a boundless world.
    The CORRECT answer is:
    A. IV, I, III, V, II B. I, V, III, IV, II C. II, I, V, III, IV D. V, IV, II, III, I

10. I. Gary King of Harvard University says that one main reason null results are not published is because there were many ways to produce them by messing up.
    II. Oddly enough, there is little hard data on how often or why null results are squelched.
    III. The various errors make the null reports almost impossible to predict, Mr. King believes.
    IV. In recent years, the debate has spread to social and behavioral science, which help sway public and social policy.
    V. The question of what to do with null results in research has long been hotly debated among those conducting medical trials.
    The CORRECT answer is:
    A. I, III, IV, V, II B. V, I, II, IV, III C. III, II, I, V, IV D. V, IV, II, I, III

11. I. In a recent study, Stanford political economist Neil Malholtra and two of his graduate students examined all studies funded by TESS (Time-sharing Experiments for Social Sciences).
    II. Scientists of these experiments cited deeper problems within their studies but also believed many journalists wouldn't be interested in their findings.
    III. TESS allows scientists to order up internet-based surveys of a representative sample of U.S. adults to test a particular hypothesis.
    IV. One scientist went on record as saying, "The reality is that null effects do not tell a clear story."
    V. Well, Malholtra's team tracked down working papers from most of the experiments that weren't published to find out what had happened to their results.
    The CORRECT answer is:
    A. IV, II, V, III, I   B. I, III, V, II, IV   C. III, V, I, IV, II   D. I, III, IV, II, V

12. I. The work also suggests that these ultra-tiny salt wires may already exist in sea spray and large underground salt deposits.
    II. Scientists expect for metals such as gold or lead to stretch out at temperatures well below their melting points, but they never expected this superplasticity in a rigid, crystalline material like salt.
    III. Inflexible old salt becomes a softy in the nanoworld, stretching like taffy to more than twice its length, researchers report.
    IV. The findings may lead to new approaches for making nanowires that could end up in solar cells or electronic circuits.
    V. According to Nathan Moore of Sandia National Laboratories, these nanowires are special and much more common than we may think.
    The CORRECT answer is:
    A. IV, III, V, II, I   B. I, V, III, IV, II   C. III, IV, I, V, II   D. V, II, III, I, IV

13. I. The Venus flytrap (Dionaea muscipula) needs to know when an ideal meal is crawling across its leaves.
    II. The large black hairs on their lobes allow the Venus flytraps to literally feel their prey, and they act as triggers that spring the trap closed.
    III. To be clear, if an insect touches just one hair, the trap will not spring shut; but a large enough bug will likely touch two hairs within twenty seconds which is the signal the Venus flytrap waits for.
    IV. Closing its trap requires a huge expense of energy, and reopening can take several hours.
    V. When the proper prey makes its way across the trap, the Dionaea launches into action.
    The CORRECT answer is:
    A. IV, I, V, II, III   B. II, V, I, III, IV   C. I, II, V, IV, III   D. I, IV, II, V, III

14. I. These books usually contain collections of stories, many of which are much older than the books themselves.
    II. Where other early European authors wrote their literary works in Latin, the Irish began writing down their stories in their own language as early as 6th century B.C.E.
    III. Ireland has the oldest vernacular literature in Europe.
    IV. One of the most famous of these collections is the epic cycle, *The Táin Bó Culainge*, which translates to "The Cattle Raid of Cooley."
    V. While much of the earliest Irish writing has been lost or destroyed, several manuscripts survive from the late medieval period.
    The CORRECT answer is:
    A. V, IV, I, II, III   B. III, II, V, I, IV   C. III, I, IV, V, II   D. IV, II, III, I, V

    14.____

15. I. Obviously the plot is thin, but it works better as a thematic peace, exploring several great issues that plagued authors and people during that era.
    II. The story begins during a raid when Meb's forces are joined by Frederick and his men.
    III. In the end, many warriors on both sides perish, the prize is lost, and peace is somehow re-established between the opposing sides.
    IV. The middle of the story tells of how Chulu fends off Meb's army by herself while Concho's men struggle against witchcraft.
    V. The prize is defended by the current king, Concho, and the young warrior, Chulu.
    The CORRECT answer is:
    A. II, V, IV, III, I   B. V, I, IV, III, II   C. I, III, V, IV, II   D. III, II, I, V, IV

    15.____

16. I. However, sometimes the flowers that are treated with the pesticides are not as vibrant as those that did not receive the treatment.
    II. The first phase featured no pesticides and the second featured a pesticide that varied in doses.
    III. In the cultivation of roses, certain pesticides are often applied when the presence of aphids is detected.
    IV. Recently, researchers conducted two phases of an experiment to study the effects of certain pesticides on rose bushes.
    V. To start, aphids are small plant-eating insects known to feed on rose bushes.
    The CORRECT answer is:
    A. IV, III, II, I, V   B. I, II, V, III, IV   C. V, III, I, IV, II   D. II, V, IV, I, III

    16.____

17. I. My passion for it took hold many years ago when I happened to cross paths with a hiker in a national park.
    II. The wilderness has a way of cleansing the spirit.
    III. His excitement was infectious as he quoted various poetic verses pertaining to the wild; I was hooked.
    IV. For some, backpacking is the ultimate vacation.
    V. While it once felt tedious and tiring, backpacking is now an essential part of my summer recreation.
    The CORRECT answer is:
    A. IV, II, V, I, III   B. II, III, I, IV, V   C. I, IV, II, V, III   D. V, I, III, II, IV

    17.____

18. I. When I was preparing for my two-week vacation to southern Africa, I realized that the continent would be like nothing I have ever seen.
    II. I wanted to explore the continent's urban streets as well as the savannah; it's always been my dream to have "off the grid" experiences as well as touristy ones.
    III. The largest gap in understanding came from an unlikely source; it was the way I played with my host family's dog.
    IV. Upon my arrival to Africa, the people I met welcomed me with open arms.
    V. Aside from the pleasant welcome, it was obvious that our cultural differences were stark, which led to plenty of laughter and confusion.
    The CORRECT answer is:
    A. IV, I, II, III, V   B. III, V, IV, II, I   C. I, IV, II, III, V   D. I, II, IV, V, III

18.____

19. I. There, I signed up for a full-contact, downhill ice-skating race that looked like a bobsled run.
    II. It wasn't until I took a trip to Montreal that I realized how wrong I was.
    III. As an avid skier and inline skater, I figured I had cornered the market on downhill speeds.
    IV. After avoiding hip and body checks, both of which were perfectly legal, I was able to reach a top speed of forty-five miles per hour!
    V. It was Carnaval season, the time when people from across the province flock to the city for two weeks of food, drink and winter sports.
    The CORRECT answer is:
    A. II, I, III, IV, V   B. III, II, V, I, IV   C. IV, V, I, III, II   D. I, IV, II, V, III

19.____

20. I. It is a spell that sets upon one's soul and a sense of euphoria is felt by all who experience it.
    II. Pictures and postcards of the Caribbean do not lie; the water there shines with every shade of aquamarine, from pastel to emerald.
    III. As I imagine these sights, I recall one trip in particular that neatly captures the allure of the Caribbean.
    IV. The ocean hypnotizes with its glassy vastness.
    V. On that beautiful day, I was incredibly happy to sail with my family and friends.
    The CORRECT answer is:
    A. I, V, IV, III, II   B. V, I, II, IV, III   C. II, IV, I, III, V   D. I, II, IV, III, V

20.____

21. I. It wasn't until the early 1700s that it began to resemble the masterpiece museum it is today.
    II. The Louvre contains some of the most famous works of art in the history of the world including the *Mona Lisa* and the *Venus de Milo*.
    III. Before it was a world famous museum, The Louvre was a fort built by King Philip sometime around 1200 A.D.
    IV. The Louvre, in Paris, France, is one of the largest museums in the world.
    V. It has almost 275,000 works of art, which are displayed in over 140 exhibition rooms.
    The CORRECT answer is:
    A. V, I, III, IV, II   B. II, IV, I, V, III   C. V, III, I, IV, II   D. IV, V, II, III, I

21.____

22. I. It danced on the glossy hair and bright eyes of two girls, who sat together hemming ruffles for a white muslin dress.
   II. The September sun was glinting cheerfully into a pretty bedroom furnished with blue.
   III. These girls were Clover and Elsie Carr, and it was Clover's first evening dress for which they were hemming ruffles.
   IV. The half-finished skirt of the dress lay on the bed, and as each crisp ruffle was completed, the girls added it to the snowy heap, which looked like a drift of transparent clouds.
   V. It was nearly two years since a certain visit made by Johnnie to Inches Mills and more than three since Clover and Katy had returned home from the boarding school at Hillsover.
   The CORRECT answer is:
   A. III, V, IV, I, II   B. II, I, IV, III, V   C. V, II, I, IV, III   D. II, IV, III, I, V

23. I. The "invisible hand" theory is harshly criticized by parties who argue that untampered self-interest is immoral and that charity is the superior vehicle for community improvement.
   II. Standing as a testament to his benevolence, Smith bequeathed much of his wealth to charity.
   III. Second, Smith was not arguing that all self-interest is positive for society; he simply did not agree that it was necessarily bad.
   IV. First, he was not declaring that people should adopt a pattern of overt self-interest, but rather that people already act in such a way.
   V. Some of these people, though, fail to recognize several important aspects of Adam Smith's the Scottish economist who championed this theory, concept.
   The CORRECT answer is:
   A. I, V, IV, III, II   B. III, IV, II, I, V   C. II, III, V, IV, I   D. IV, III, I, V, II

24. I. Though they rarely are awarded for their many accomplishments, composers and performers continue to innovate and represent a substantial reason for classical music's persistent popularity.
   II. It is often the subject of experimentation on the part of composers and performers.
   III. Even more restrictive is the mainstream definition of "classical," which only includes the music of generations past that has seemingly been pushed aside by such contemporary forms of music as jazz, rock, and rap.
   IV. In spite of its waning limelight, however, classical music occupies an enduring niche in Western culture.
   V. Many people take classical music to be the realm of the symphony orchestra or smaller ensembles of orchestral instruments.
   The CORRECT answer is:
   A. IV, I, III, II, V   B. II, IV, V, I, III   C. V, III, IV, II, I   D. I, V, III, IV, II

25. I. The Great Pyramid at Giza is arguably one of the most fascinating and contentious pieces of architecture in the world.
  II. Instead of clarifying or expunging older theories about its age, the results of the study left the researchers mystified.
  III. In the 1980s, researchers began focusing on studying the mortar from the pyramid, hoping it would reveal important clues about the pyramid's age and construction.
  IV. This discovery was controversial because these dates claimed that the structure was built over 400 years earlier than most archaeologists originally believed it had been constructed.
  V. Carbon dating revealed that the pyramid had been built between 3100 BCE and 2850 BCE with an average date of 2977 BCE.
  The CORRECT answer is:
   A. I, III, II, V, IV   B. II, III, IV, V, I   C. V, I, III, IV, II   D. III, IV, V, I, II

KEY (CORRECT ANSWERS)

1.	C		11.	B
2.	A		12.	C
3.	D		13.	D
4.	B		14.	B
5.	B		15.	A
6.	C		16.	C
7.	A		17.	A
8.	D		18.	D
9.	A		19.	B
10.	D		20.	C

21.	D
22.	B
23.	A
24.	C
25.	A

EXAMINATION SECTION
TEST 1

DIRECTIONS: The sentences listed below are part of a meaningful paragraph, but they are not given in their proper order. You are to decide what would be the BEST order to put sentences to form a well-organized paragraph. Each sentence has a place in the paragraph; there are no extra sentences. *PRINT THE LETTER OF THE CORRECT ANSWER IN THE SPACE AT THE RIGHT.*

Questions 1-3.

DIRECTIONS: Questions 1 through 3 are to be answered on the basis of the following passage.

Almost half of the increase in Chicago came from five neighborhoods, including West Garfield Park. He was 12 years old and had just been recruited into a gang by his older brothers and cousin. A decade later, he sits in Cook County jail, held without bail and awaiting trial on three cases, including felony drug charges and possession of a weapon. Violence in Chicago erupted last year, with the city recording 771 murders—a 58% jump from 2015. They point to a $95 million police-training center in West Garfield Park, public-transit improvements on Chicago's south side and efforts to get major corporations such as Whole Foods and Wal-Mart to invest. Chicago city officials say that they are making strategic investments in ailing neighborhoods. Amarley Coggins remembers the first time he dealt heroin, discreetly approaching a car coming off an interstate highway and into West Garfield park, the neighborhood where he grew up on Chicago's west side.

1. When organized correctly, the first sentence of the paragraph begins with   1.____
   A. "Amarley Coggins remembers…" B. "He was 12 years old…"
   C. "They point to a…"   D. "Violence in Chicago…"

2. After correctly organizing the paragraph, the author wishes to replace a word   2.____
   in the last sentence with its synonym *enterprises*. Which word does the author wish to replace?
   A. murders   B. neighborhoods
   C. corporations   D. improvements

3. If put together correctly, the second to last sentence would end with the words   3.____
   A. "…Chicago's west side."   B. "…in ailing neighborhoods."
   C. "…older brother and cousins."   D. "…and Wal-Mart to invest."

Questions 4-6.

DIRECTIONS: Questions 4 through 6 are to be answered on the basis of the following passage.

Critics argue that driverless vehicles pose too many risks, including cyberattacks, computer malfunctions, relying on algorithms to make ethical decisions, and fewer transportation jobs. Driverless vehicles, also called autonomous vehicles and self-driving vehicles, are vehicles that can operate without human intervention. And algorithms make decisions based on data obtained from sensors and connectivity. Driverless vehicles rely primarily on three technologies: sensors, connectivity, and algorithms. Sensors observe multiple directions simultaneously. Connectivity accesses information on traffic, weather, road hazards, and navigation. Supporters argue that driverless vehicles have many benefits, including fewer traffic accidents and fatalities, more efficient traffic flows, greater mobility for those who cannot drive, and less pollution. Once the realm of science fiction, driverless vehicles could revolutionize automotive travel over the next few decades.

4. When all of the sentences are organized in correct order, the first sentence starts with
   A. "Connectivity accesses information…"
   B. "Critics argue that…"
   C. "Once the realm of…"
   D. "Driverless vehicles, also called…"

4._____

5. If the above paragraph appeared in correct order, which of the following transition words would be MOST appropriate in the beginning of the sentence that starts "Critics argue that…"
   A. Additionally
   B. To begin,
   C. In conclusion,
   D. Conversely,

5._____

6. When the paragraph is properly arranged, it ends with the words
   A. "…over the next few decades."
   B. "…fewer transportation jobs."
   C. "…and less pollution."
   D. "…without human intervention"

6._____

Questions 7-10.

DIRECTIONS: Questions 7 through 10 are to be answered on the basis of the following passage.

This method had some success, but also carried fatal risks. Various people across Europe independently developed vaccination as an alternative during the later years of the eighteenth century, but Edward Jenner (1749-1823) popularized the practice. Vaccination has been called a miracle of modern medicine, but it has a long and controversial history stretching back to the ancient world. In 1803 the Royal Jennerian Institute was founded in England, and vaccination programs initially drew enormous public support. In 429 BCE in Greece, the historian Thucydides (c.460-c.395 BCE) noted that survivors of smallpox did not become reinfected in subsequent epidemics. Variolation as a means of preventing severe smallpox infection became an accepted practice in China in the tenth century CE, and its popularity spread across Asia,

Europe, and to the Americas by the seventeenth century. Variolation required either inhalation of smallpox dust, or putting scabs or parts of the smallpox pustules under the skin. Widespread inoculation against smallpox was purported to have been part of Ayurvedic tradition as far back as at least 1000 BCE, when Indian doctors traveled to households before the rainy season each year.

7. When arranged properly, what does "This method" refer to in the sentence that begins "This method had some success…"? 7.____
    A. Vaccination
    B. Inoculation
    C. Variolation
    D. Hybridization

8. When organized correctly, the paragraph's third sentence should begin 8.____
    A. "In 429 BCE in Greece…"
    B. "Variolation required…"
    C. "In 1803 the…"
    D. "Vaccination has been called…"

9. If put in the correct order, this paragraph should end with the words 9.____
    A. "…under the skin."
    B. "…to the ancient world."
    C. "…enormous public support."
    D. "…by the seventeenth century."

10. In the second sentence, the author is thinking about using the word immunization instead of which of its synonyms? 10.____
    A. Variolation   B. Vaccination   C. Inhalation   D. Inoculation

Questions 11-13.

DIRECTIONS: Questions 11 through 13 are to be answered on the basis of the following passage.

Summers are hot—often north of 100 degrees—and because it lies at the far end of a San Diego Gas & Electric transmission line, the town has suffered frequent power outages. Another way is that microgrids can ease the entry of intermittent renewable energy sources, like wind and solar, into the modern grid. Utilities are also interested in microgrids because of the money they can save by deferring the need to build new transmission lines. "If you're on the very end of a utility line, everything that happens, happens 10 times worse for you," says Mike Gravely, team leader for energy systems integration at the California Energy Commission. The town has a lot of senior citizens, who can be frail in the heat. Borrego Springs, California, is a quaint town of about 3,400 people set against the Anza-Borrego Desert about 90 miles east of San Diego. High winds, lightning strikes, forest fires and flash floods can bust up that line and kill the electricity. But today, Borrego Springs has a failsafe against power outages: a microgrid. Resiliency is one of the main reasons the market in microgrids is booming, with installed capacity in the United States projected to be more than double between 2017 and 2022, according to a new report on microgrids from GTM Research. "Without air conditioning," says Linda Haddock, head of the local Chamber of Commerce, "people will die."

11. When the sentences above are organized correctly, the paragraph should start with the sentence that begins 11.____
    A. "Borrego Springs, California…"
    B. "But today, Borrego Springs…"
    C. "Summers are hot…"
    D. "Utilities are also interested…"

12. If the author wanted to split this paragraph into two smaller paragraphs, the first sentence of the second paragraph would start with the words
    A. "High winds, lightning strikes, forest fires…"
    B. "But today, Borrego Springs…"
    C. "Resiliency is one of the main…"
    D. "If you're on the very end…"

    12.____

13. Assuming the paragraph were organized correctly, the second to last sentence would end
    A. "…to build new transmission lines."
    B. "…be frail in the heat."
    C. "…into the modern grid."
    D. "…east of San Diego."

    13.____

Questions 14-17.

DIRECTIONS: Questions 14 through 17 are to be answered on the basis of the following passage.

Exhaustive search is not typically a successful approach to problem solving because most interesting problems have search spaces that are simply too large to be dealt with in this manner, even by the fastest computers. Thus, in order to ignore a portion of a search space, some guiding knowledge or insight must exist so that the solution will not be overlooked. This partial understanding is reflected in the fact that a rigid algorithmic solution—a routine and predetermined number of computational steps—cannot be applied. A large part of the intelligence of chess players resides in the heuristics they employ. When search is used to explore the entire solution space, it is said to be exhaustive. Chess is a classic example where humans routinely employ sophisticated heuristics in a search space. Therefore, if one hopes to find a solution (or a reasonably good approximation of a solution) to such a problem, one must selectively explore the problem's search space. Rather, the concept of search is used to solve such problems. Heuristics is a major area of AI that concerns itself with how to limit effectively the exploration of a search space. Many problems that humans are confronted with are not fully understood. The difficulty here is that if part of the search space is not explored, one runs the risk that the solution one seeks will be missed. A chess player will typically search through a small number of possible moves before selecting a move to play. Not every possible move and countermove sequence is explored. Only reasonable sequences are examined.

14. When correctly organized, the paragraph above should begin with the words
    A. "Many problems that…"
    B. "Therefore, if one hopes to…"
    C. "Only reasonable sequences are…"
    D. "The difficulty here is…"

    14.____

15. If the paragraph was organized correctly, the fourth sentence would begin with the words
    A. "Chess is a classic…"   B. "Heuristics is a major…"
    C. "Exhaustive search is not…"   D. "The difficulty here is…"

    15.____

16. If the author wished to separate this paragraph into two equally sized paragraphs, the sentence that begins the second paragraph would END with the words
    A. "...heuristics they employ."
    B. "...in a search space."
    C. "...are not fully employed."
    D. "...will be missed."

17. When organized correctly, the paragraph would end with the words
    A. "...the heuristics they employ."
    B. "...will not be overlooked."
    C. "...said to be exhaustive."
    D. "...are not fully understood."

Questions 18-21.

DIRECTIONS: Questions 18 through 21 are to be answered on the basis of the following passage.

Asian-Americans soon found themselves the targets of ridicule and attacks. Prior to the bombing he had tried to enlist in the military but was turned down due to poor health. His case, Korematsu v. The United States, is still considered a blemish on the record of the Supreme Court and has received heightened scrutiny given the indefinite confinement of many prisoners after the terrorist attacks on September 11, 2001. On February 19, 1942, President Franklin D. Roosevelt issued Executive Order 9066, which granted the leaders of the armed forces permission to create Military Areas and authorizing the removal of any and all persons from those areas. Fred Korematsu was a 22-year-old welder when the Japanese bombed Pearl Harbor on December 7, 1941. A Nisei—which means an American citizen born to Japanese parents—he was one of four brothers and grew up working in his parents' plant nursery in Oakland, California. This statement effectively pronounced Japanese-Americans on the West Coast as traitors because even though Executive Order 9066 allowed the military to remove any person from designated areas, only those of Japanese descent were ordered to leave. Before Pearl Harbor, he was employed by a defense contractor in California. At the time of the attack, he was having a picnic with his Italian-American girlfriend. Asian-American Fred Korematsu (1919-2005) is most remembered for challenging the legality of Japanese internment during World War II. It was for this simple reason that he eventually became known as a civil rights leader. American reaction to an attack on United States' soil was both swift and harsh. Awarded the Presidential Medal of Honor, he is considered a leader of the civil rights movement in the United States. Roosevelt justified these actions in the opening paragraph of the order by declaring, "the successful prosecution of the war requires every possible protection against espionage, and against sabotage to national-defense material, national-defenses premises and national-defense utilities." Years later he told the San Francisco Chronicle, "I was just living my life, and that's what I wanted to do."

18. When put together correctly, the above paragraph would begin with the words
    A. "It was for this simple reason..."
    B. "A Nisei—which means..."
    C. "Awarded the Presidential Medal of Honor..."
    D. "Asian-American Fred Korematsu..."

19. If the author wished to separate this piece into two separate paragraphs, the sentence that would be the BEST way to start the second paragraph would begin with the words
    A. "Awarded the Presidential Medal of Honor…"
    B. "Fred Korematsu was a…"
    C. "Roosevelt justified these actions…"
    D. "Before Pearl Harbor, he was…"

20. In the sentence that begins "A Nisei—which means…", who does "he" refer to in the paragraph?
    A. Roosevelt
    B. A sibling of Korematsu
    C. Fred Korematsu
    D. Japanese-Americans on the West Coast

21. If organized correctly, the fourth sentence should begin with the words
    A. "At the time of the attack…"
    B. "His case, Korematsu v. The United States…"
    C. "Fred Korematsu was a…"
    D. "This statement effectively pronounced…"

22. When put together correctly, the last sentence of the paragraph should end with the words
    A. "…that's what I wanted to do."
    B. "…were ordered to leave."
    C. "…during World War II."
    D. "…was both swift and harsh."

Questions 23-25.

DIRECTIONS: Questions 23 through 25 are to be answered on the basis of the following passage.

Over the past two decades, her personal finances have been eroded by illness, divorce, the cost of raising two children, the housing bust, and the economic downturn. "There are more people attending college, more people taking out loans, and more people taking out a higher dollar amount of loans," says Matthew Ward, associate director of media relations at the New York Fed. Anderson, who is 57, told her complicated story at a recent Senate Aging Committee hearing (she's previously appeared on the CBS Evening News). Some 3 percent of U.S. households that are headed by a senior citizen now hold federal student debt, mostly debt they took on to finance their own educations, according to a new report from the Government Accountability Office (GAO), an independent agency. She hasn't been able to afford payments on her loans for nearly eight years. Rosemary Anderson has a master's degree, a good job at the University of California (Santa Cruz), and student loans that she could be paying off until she's 81. Student debt has risen across every age group over the past decade, according to a Federal Reserve Bank of New York analysis of credit report data… "As the baby boomers continue to move into retirement, the number of older Americans with defaulted loans will only continue to increase," the report warned. She first enrolled in college in her thirties.

23. When organized correctly, the first sentence should begin with the words
    A. "She first enrolled…"
    B. "Anderson, who is 57…"
    C. "Some 3 percent of…"
    D. "Rosemary Anderson has…"

24. If the author wished to split the paragraph into two paragraphs (not necessarily equal in length), the first sentence of the second paragraph would begin with the words
    A. "Some 3 percent of…"
    B. "There are more people…"
    C. "Over the past two decades…"
    D. "She first enrolled…"

25. When put in the correct order, the second to last sentence should end with the words
    A. "…an independent agency."
    B. "…of credit report data."
    C. "…at the New York Fed."
    D. "…in her thirties."

KEY (CORRECT ANSWERS)

1.	A		11.	A
2.	C		12.	B
3.	B		13.	C
4.	D		14.	A
5.	D		15.	C
6.	B		16.	D
7.	C		17.	A
8.	A		18.	D
9.	C		19.	B
10.	D		20.	C

21.	C
22.	B
23.	D
24.	A
25.	B

TEST 2

DIRECTIONS: The sentences listed below are part of a meaningful paragraph, but they are not given in their proper order. You are to decide what would be the BEST order to put sentences to form a well-organized paragraph. Each sentence has a place in the paragraph; there are no extra sentences. *PRINT THE LETTER OF THE CORRECT ANSWER IN THE SPACE AT THE RIGHT.*

Questions 1-3.

DIRECTIONS: Questions 1 through 3 are to be answered on the basis of the following passage.

According to the World Health Organization (WHO), exposure to ambient (outdoor) air pollution causes 3 million premature deaths around the world each year, largely due to heart and lung diseases. Air pollution also contributes to such environmental threats as smog, acid rain, depletion of the ozone layer, and global climate change. The U.S. Environmental Protection Agency (EPA) sets National Ambient Air Quality Standards (NAAQS) for those four pollutants as well as carbon monoxide (CO) and lead. The EPA also regulates 187 toxic air pollutants, such as asbestos, benzene, dioxin, and mercury. Finally, the EPA places limits on emissions of greenhouse gases like carbon dioxide (CO_2) and methane, which contribute to global climate change. The WHO has established Air Quality Guidelines (ACGs) to identify safe levels of exposure to the emission of four harmful air pollutants worldwide: particulate matter (PM), ozone (O_3), nitrogen dioxide (NO_2), and sulfur dioxide (SO_2). Since EPA criteria define the allowable concentrations of these six substances in ambient air throughout the United States, they are known as criteria air pollutants. Air pollution refers to the release into the air of chemicals and other substances, known as pollutants, that are potentially harmful to human health and the environment.

1. When organized correctly, the first sentence of this paragraph should begin
   A. "Air pollution refers…"
   B. "The EPA also regulates..,"
   C. "The WHO has established…"
   D. "According to the…"

2. When put in the correct order, the fourth sentence should end with the words
   A. "…to global climate change."
   B. "…as criteria air pollutants."
   C. "…nitrogen dioxide (NO_2), and sulfur dioxide (SO_2)."
   D. "…health and the environment."

3. If put in the most logical order, the paragraph would end with the words
   A. "…as criteria air pollutants."
   B. "…to global climate change."
   C. "…benzene, dioxin, and mercury."
   D. "…human health and the environment."

Questions 4-6.

DIRECTIONS: Questions 4 through 6 are to be answered on the basis of the following passage.

Although gentrification has been associated with some positive impacts, such as urban revitalization and lower crime rates, critics charge that it marginalizes racial and ethnic minorities and destroys the character of urban neighborhoods. British sociologist Ruth Glass is credited with coining the term "gentrification" in her 1964 book *London: Aspects of Change*, which described the transformation that occurred when members of the gentry (an elite or privileged social class) took over working-class districts of London. Gentrification is a type of neighborhood change, a broader term that encompasses various physical, demographic, social, and economic processes that affect distinct residential areas. The arrival of wealthier people leads to new economic development and an increase in property values and rent, which often makes housing unaffordable for longtime residents. Gentrification is a transformation process that typically occurs in urban neighborhoods when higher-income people move in and displace lower-income existing residents.

4. When organized in the correct order, the first sentence of the paragraph should begin with the words
   A. "Gentrification is a type of…"
   B. "British sociologist Ruth…"
   C. "The arrival of…"
   D. "Gentrification is a transformation…"

4.____

5. If put together in the correct order, the second to last sentence in the paragraph would end with the words
   A. "…lower-income existing residents."
   B. "…that affect distinct residential areas."
   C. "…character of urban neighborhoods."
   D. "…working-class districts of London."

5.____

6. If the author wished to change the beginning of the final sentence to "in the end." to better signal the finish of the paragraph, which of the following words would the phrase appear in front of?
   A. British
   B. Gentrification
   C. Although
   D. The

6.____

Questions 7-11.

DIRECTIONS: Questions 7 through 11 are to be answered on the basis of the following passage.

The primary signs of ADHD include a persistent pattern of inattention or hyperactivity lasting in duration for six months or longer with an onset before 12 years of age. Children with ADHD often experience peer rejection, neglect, or teasing and family interactions may contain high levels of discord and negative interactions (APA, 2013). Two primary types of the disorder include inattentive and hyperactive/impulsive, with a combined type when both inattention and hyperactivity occur together. Inattentive ADHD is evidenced by executive functioning deficits such as being off task, lacking sustained focus, and being disorganized. Hyperactive ADHD is evidenced by excessive talkativeness and fidgeting, with an inability to control impulses that may result in harm. Attention Deficit Hyperactivity Disorder (ADHD) is a commonly diagnosed childhood behavioral disorder affecting millions of children in the U.S. every year (National Institute of Mental Health [NIMH], 2012), with prevalence rates between 5% and 11% of the population. Other research has examined singular traits such as executive function deficits in the school setting, task performance in the school setting (Berk, 1986), driving and awareness of time. However, researching academic aspects of the school experience does not provide a comprehensive understanding of the systemic effects of ADHD in the school environment. Historically, much research on ADHD has focused on the academic impact of behavioral symptoms such as reading and mathematics. These behaviors are inappropriate for the child's age level and symptoms typically interfere with functioning in multiple environments.

7. If the author put the paragraph into a logical order, the first sentence would begin with the words
   A. "Inattentive ADHD is…"
   B. "Historically, much research…"
   C. "These behaviors are…"
   D. "Attention Deficit Hyperactivity Disorder…"

7.____

8. When put in the correct order, what does the author mean by "These behaviors" in the sentence that begins "These behaviors are…"?
   A. Inattention or hyperactivity   B. Reading and Mathematics
   C. Peer rejection   D. Sustained focus

8.____

9. If the author wished to split this paragraph into two paragraphs (not necessarily equal parts), the first sentence of the second paragraph would BEGIN with the words
   A. "Historically, much research…"
   B. "Other research has examined…"
   C. "Two primary types of…"
   D. "Inattentive ADHD is evidenced…"

9.____

10. When put in the correct order, the third sentence in the paragraph would END with the words
    A. "…an onset before 12 years of age."
    B. "…5% and 11% of the population."
    C. "…such as reading and mathematics."
    D. "…in multiple environments."

10.____

11. If the above paragraph was organized correctly, its ending words of the last sentence would be
    A. "…sustained focus, and being disorganized."
    B. "…an onset before 12 years of age."
    C. "…in the school environment."
    D. "…inattention and hyperactivity occur together."

11.____

Questions 12-15.

DIRECTIONS: Questions 12 through 15 are to be answered on the basis of the following passage.

Health care fraud imposes huge costs on society. In prosecutions of fraud, the DOJ employs the resources of its own criminal and civil divisions, as well as those of the U.S. Attorneys' Offices, HHS, and the FBI. The FBI estimates that health care fraud accounts for at least three and possibly up to ten percent of total health care expenditures, or somewhere between $82 billion and $272 billion each year. Providers are also careful to screen hires for excluded persons or entities lest they be subject to civil monetary penalties. Several government agencies are involved in fighting health care fraud. Individual states assist the HHS Office of the Inspector General ("OIG") and Centers for Medicare & Medicaid Services ("CMS") to initiate and pursue investigations of Medicare and Medicaid fraud. In addition, the OIG uses its permissive exclusion authority to exclude individuals and entities convicted of health care related crimes from federally funded health care services in order to induce providers to help track fraud through a voluntary disclosure program. $30 to $98 billion dollars of that (approximately 36%) is fraud against the public health programs Medicare and Medicaid. The Department of Justice ("DOJ") and the Department of Health and Human Services ("HHS") enforce federal health care fraud law and regulations.

12. When put together in a logical order, the second sentence of the paragraph would end with the words
    A. "...in fighting health care fraud."
    B. "...$272 billion each year."
    C. "...voluntary disclosure program."
    D. "...to civil monetary penalties."

13. In order to organize the paragraph correctly, the sentence that begins "In addition, the OIG..." should FOLLOW the sentence that begins with the words
    A. "$30 to $98 billion dollars of that..."
    B. "Health care fraud..."
    C. "Individual states assist..."
    D. "In prosecutions of fraud..."

14. The author wishes to split the paragraph into a smaller introductory paragraph followed by a slightly longer body paragraph. Which of the following sentences would be BEST to start the second paragraph?
    A. "$30 to $98 billion dollars of that (approximately 36%) is fraud against the public health care programs Medicare and Medicaid."
    B. "Several government agencies are involved in fighting health care fraud."
    C. "In prosecutions of fraud, the DOJ employs the resources of its own criminal and civil divisions, as well as those of the U.S. Attorneys' Offices, HHS, and the FBI."
    D. "Health care fraud imposes huge costs on society."

15. If put together correctly, the paragraph should end with the words   15._____
    A. "...Attorneys' Offices, HHS, and the FBI."
    B. "...huge costs on society."
    C. "...fighting health care fraud."
    D. "...of Medicare and Medicaid fraud."

Questions 16-19.

DIRECTIONS: Questions 16 through 19 are to be answered on the basis of the following passage.

President Abraham Lincoln advocated for granting amnesty to former Confederates to heal the country after the devastating war. Adams and his fellow Federalist Party members in Congress used the law to jail more than a dozen of his political rivals. In 1977, President Jimmy Carter lifted the restrictions on draft dodgers, granting them unconditional amnesty. The issue of amnesty again arose shortly after the U.S. Civil War (1861-1865). Some U.S. government officials, including Vice President Andrew Johnson, advocating placing severe punishments on the military and civilian leaders of the secessionist Confederate States of America. A century later, the controversial nature of the Vietnam War (1964-1975), combined with the compulsory draft for military service, compelled many young men of eligible age to violate the law to avoid the draft. When Thomas Jefferson, Adams' Vice President and opponent of the Alien and Sedition Acts, won the 1800 presidential election, he declared amnesty for those found to have violated the law. Other young men who were drafted deserted the army and refused to serve. In May 1865, when serving as president following Lincoln's assassination, Johnson issued the Proclamation of Amnesty and Reconstruction, which granted the rights of voting and holding office to most former Confederates. In 1974, President Gerald Ford granted amnesty to deserters and "draft dodgers" on the condition that they swear allegiance to the United States and engage in two years of community service. In 1798, President John Adams signed the Alien and Sedition Acts, a set of four laws that restricted criticism of the federal government.

16. When put in the correct order, the paragraph would begin with the following words.   16._____
    A. "Some U.S. government..."   B. "In May 1865, when..."
    C. "A century later, the..."   D. "In 1798, President..."

17. If put in logical order, what sentence number would the sentence that begins   17._____
    "President Abraham Lincoln..." be?
    A. One   B. Six   C. Five   D. Two

18. The author wants to split this paragraph into three separate paragraphs. The   18._____
    THIRD paragraph should begin with the words
    A. "The issue of amnesty again..."   B. "In 1798, President..."
    C. "In 1977, President Jimmy..."   D. "A century later, the..."

19. When organized in sequential order, the last sentence of the paragraph   19._____
    would end with the words
    A. "...of his political rivals."   B. "...after the devastating war."
    C. "...them unconditional amnesty."   D. "...of the federal government."

Questions 20-22.

DIRECTIONS: Questions 20 through 22 are to be answered on the basis of the following passage.

Throughout history, militias have played an important role in national defense against foreign invaders or oppressors. In the original American colonies, state militias served to keep order and played an important role in the fight for independence from the British during the American Revolutionary War. Since that time, state-level militias have continued to exist in the United States alongside a national standing army, providing additional reserve defense and emergency assistance when needed. Some countries still rely almost entirely on public militias for civil defense. In Switzerland, for example, all able-bodied males must serve as part of the Swiss military or civilian service for several months starting when they turn 20 years old and remain reserve militia for years after. Similarly, in Israel, all non-Arab citizens over the age of 18 are required to serve in the Israel Defense Forces for at least two years; Israel is unique in that it requires military service from female citizens as well as males.

20. When put into the correct order, the paragraph should begin with the words 20.____
    A. "Throughout history, militias..."   B. "Similarly, in Israel..."
    C. "Some countries still rely..."   D. "Since that time, state-level..."

21. The fifth sentence of the paragraph should end with the words 21.____
    A. "...against foreign invaders or oppressors."
    B. "...militias for civil defense."
    C. "...reserve militia for years after."
    D. "...citizens as well as males."

22. The last sentence of the paragraph should end with the words 22.____
    A. "...militias for civil defense."
    B. "...citizens as well as males."
    C. "...against foreign invaders or oppressors."
    D. "...during the American Revolutionary War."

Questions 23-25.

DIRECTIONS: Questions 23 through 25 are to be answered on the basis of the following passage.

Medicines such as herbal and homeopathic remedies differ radically from those typically prescribed by mainstream physicians. These practices derive from different cultural traditions and scientific premises. As of 2012, the Memorial Sloan-Kettering Cancer Center offered hypnosis and tai chi, which is an ancient Chinese exercise, to help eases the pains associated with conventional cancer treatments. Some medical professionals staunchly dismiss a number of alternative techniques and theories as quackery. The concept of alternative medicine encompasses an extremely wide range of therapeutic modalities, from acupuncture to yoga. As of 2012, nearly 40 percent of Americans use some alternative medicines or therapies, according to the National Institutes of Health's National Center for Complementary and Alternative Medicine. Alternative approaches to health, fitness, disease prevention, and treatment are sometimes referred to as holistic health care or natural medicine. These names suggest some of the philosophical foundations shared by traditions such as homeopathy, naturopathy, traditional Chinese medicine and herbal medicine. A University of Pennsylvania study in 2010 found that more than 70 percent of U.S. cancer centers offered information on complementary therapies. Increasingly, health care providers are encouraging patients to combine alternative and conventional (or allopathic) treatments, a practice known as complementary or integrative medicine. In the contemporary United States, the phrase alternative medicine has come to mean virtually any healing or wellness practice not based within the conventional system of medical doctors, nurses, and hospitals. Some of these alternative treatments include acupuncture to alleviate pain and nausea and yoga to help reduce stress and manage pain. Yet taken as a whole, the alternative sector of the health field is enormously popular and rapidly growing. The Health Services Research Journal reported in 2011 that three out of four U.S. health care workers used complementary or alternative medicine practices themselves. Other studies have shown that more medical professionals are recommending that cancer patients seek alternative treatments to deal with the side effects of conventional treatments, such as chemotherapy, radiation, and surgery.

23. When put in the correct order, the first sentence should begin with the words
    A. "A University of Pennsylvania study…"
    B. "Other studies have shown that…"
    C. "Increasingly, health care providers…"
    D. "In the contemporary United States…"

24. If the author were to split the paragraph into two separate ones, the first sentence of the second paragraph should begin with the words
    A. "Alternative approaches to health…"
    B. "The concept of alternative medicine…"
    C. "As of 2012, nearly 40%..."
    D. "These names suggest some…"

25. When put into the correct logical sequence, the paragraph should end with the words
    A. "…Complementary and Alternative Medicine."
    B. "…system of medical doctors, nurses, and hospitals."
    C. "…associated with conventional cancer treatments."
    D. "…health care or natural medicine."

KEY (CORRECT ANSWERS)

1.	A		11.	C
2.	C		12.	B
3.	B		13.	C
4.	D		14.	B
5.	B		15.	A
6.	C		16.	D
7.	D		17.	B
8.	A		18.	D
9.	A		19.	C
10.	D		20.	A

21.	C
22.	B
23.	D
24.	A
25.	C

PREPARING WRITTEN MATERIAL
PARAGRAPH REARRANGEMENT

EXAMINATION SECTION
TEST 1

DIRECTIONS: The sentences listed below are part of a meaningful paragraph, but they are not given in their proper order. You are to decide what would be the BEST order to put sentences to form a well-organized paragraph. Each sentence has a place in the paragraph; there are no extra sentences. *PRINT THE LETTER OF THE CORRECT ANSWER IN THE SPACE AT THE RIGHT.*

1.
   I. That robots and software can replace people might seem obvious to anyone who's worked as a travel agent or in automotives.
   II. Even more ominous for workers, they foresee dismal prospects for many types of jobs as these powerful new technologies are increasingly adopted not only in manufacturing but in professions such as education and medicine.
   III. Scholars Erik Brynjolfsson and Andrew McAfee have argued that impressive advances in computer technology are largely behind the sluggish employment growth of the last 10 to 15 years.
   IV. They believe that rapid technology change has been destroying jobs faster than it is creating them.
   V. However, Brynjolfsson and McAfee's claim is more troubling and controversial.
   The CORRECT answer is:
   A. II, V, IV, III, I   B. V, I, III, IV, II   C. III, II, I, V, IV   D. IV, III, V, II, I

   1.____

2.
   I. While technological changes can be painful for workers whose skills no longer match the needs of employers, Lawrence Katz, a Harvard economist, says that no historical pattern shows these shifts leading to a net decrease in jobs over an extended period.
   II. There is no long-term trend of eliminating work for people.
   III. Over the long term, employment rates are fairly stable.
   IV. While it can take decades for workers to acquire the expertise needed for new types of employment, he says, "We never have run out of jobs."
   V. Katz has done extensive research on how technological advances have affected jobs over the last few centuries—describing, for example, how highly skilled artisans in the mid-19th century were displaced by lower-skilled workers in factories.
   The CORRECT answer is:
   A. V, I, III, IV, II   B. I, V, IV, II, III   C. III, V, II, I, IV   D. IV, II, V, III, I

   2.____

3.
   I. There are two reasons birds might fly in a V formation: It may make flight easier, or they're simply following the leader.
   II. Models that treated flapping birds like fixed-wing airplanes estimate that they save energy by drafting off each other, but currents created by airplanes are far more stable than the oscillating eddies coming off of a bird.

   3.____

III. Squadrons of planes can save fuel by flying in a V formation, and many scientists suspect that migrating birds do the same.
IV. A new study of ibises finds that these big-winged birds carefully position their wingtips and sync their flapping, presumably to catch the preceding bird's updraft—and save energy during flight.
V. Anyone watching the autumn sky knows that migrating birds fly in a V formation, but scientists have long debated why.
The CORRECT answer is:
   A. V, IV, I, III, II   B. V, IV, III, II, I   C. I, V, II, IV, III   D. III, IV, V, I, II

4. I. It may readily be conceived, that by thus attempting to make one sex equal to the other both are degraded.
II. There are people in Europe who, confounding together the different characteristics of the sexes, would make of man and woman beings not only equal but alike.
III. Their occupations, their pleasures, their business would all be conflated.
IV. They would give to both the same functions, impose on both the same duties, and grant to both the same rights; they would mix them in all things.
V. From so preposterous a medley of the works of nature, nothing could ever result but weak men and disorderly women.
The CORRECT answer is:
   A. I, II, III, V, IV   B. IV, I, III, II, V   C. V, IV, I, III, II   D. II, IV, III, I, V

5. I. However, when the feelings become overwhelming and last for weeks or months, professional treatment can help.
II. If untreated, depression can lead to social withdrawal, physical complaints, such as fatigue, sleep problems, aches and pains, and even suicide.
III. According to the American Psychiatric Association, 80 to 90 percent of people with depression can be helped.
IV. Everyone feels sad, blue, or discouraged occasionally, but usually those feelings do not interfere with everyday life and do not need treatment.
V. Depression is one of the most common and serious mental disorders; however, it is also one of the most treatable.
The CORRECT answer is:
   A. IV, I, V, III, II   B. V, II, III, I, IV   C. II, III, V, IV, I   D. I, III, IV, V, II

6. I. A swampy region in southern Florida, the Everglades, are described as a vast, shallow sawgrass marsh with tree islands, wet prairies, and aquatic sloughs.
II. The Everglades historically covered most of southeastern Florida, prior to massive drainage and reclamation projects launched at the beginning of the twentieth century.
III. The glades constitute the southern end of the Kissimmee Lake Okeechobee Everglades system, which encompasses most of south and central Florida below Orlando.
IV. Today, intensive agriculture in the north and rapid urban development in the east are among the Everglades' various land uses.

V. Originally, the Everglades covered an area approximately forty miles (64 km) wide and one hundred miles (161 km) long, or 2.5 million acres (1 million hectares), but large segments have been isolated by canals and levees.

The CORRECT answer is:

A. IV, V, I, II, III   B. III, IV, V, II, I   C. I, II, III, V, IV   D. V, IV, III, I, II

7.
I. She is well respected within the scientific community for her groundbreaking field studies and is credited with the first recorded observation of chimps eating meat and using and making tools.
II. In 2014, she published a book on botany, sharing her lifetime love for the mysteries and potential that plants hold.
III. Jane Goodall is known worldwide for her studies of the chimpanzees of the Gombe Stream Reserve in Tanzania, Africa.
IV. Because of Goodall's discoveries, scientists have been forced to redefine the characteristics once considered as solely human traits.
V. Even at the age of 80, Goodall continued to lead efforts to ensure that animals were treated humanely both in their wild habitats and in captivity.

The CORRECT answer is:

A. III, II, I, V, IV   B. III, I, IV, V, II   C. I, III, V, IV, II   D. V, II, I, III, IV

8.
I. This could be an important water source in many drought-prone areas.
II. This is due to polluted water and water-borne diseases such as cholera, polio, dysentery, and typhoid.
III. Whether by distillation or by reverse osmosis, desalination of water can transform water that is unusable because of its salinity into valuable fresh water.
IV. The World Health Organization (WHO) estimates that only two in five people in the less-developed countries (LDCs) have access to safe drinking water.
V. The WHO also estimates that at least 25 million people of the LDCs die each year.

The CORRECT answer is:

A. V, I, III, II, IV   B. I, IV, V, III, II   C. II, III, V, I, IV   D. IV, V, II, III, I

9.
I. They move randomly in all directions and bounce around and into each other.
II. Gas and liquid molecules are always in motion.
III. As they move, molecules have a tendency to spread out, moving from areas with many molecules to areas with fewer molecules.
IV. If you opened a bottle of vanilla in your kitchen, for example, you probably could soon smell the vanilla in all parts of the room, which is one example of diffusion.
V. This process of spreading out is called diffusion.

The CORRECT answer is:

A. I, III, IV, V, II   B. III, IV, I, II, V   C. V, II, III, IV, I   D. II, I, V, III, IV

10.
   I. Metabolism refers to the highly integrated network of chemical reactions by which living cells grow and sustain themselves.
   II. Anabolism uses energy stored in the form of adenosine triphosphate (ATP) to build larger molecules from smaller molecules.
   III. Catabolic reactions degrade larger molecules in order to produce ATP and raw materials for anabolic reactions.
   IV. This network is composed of two major types of pathways: anabolism and catabolism.
   V. Together, these two general metabolic networks have three major functions.
   The CORRECT answer is:
   A. V, IV, I, III, II   B. I, IV, II, III, V   C. IV, I, II, III, V   D. III, V, IV, II, I

10.____

11.
   I. The resurgence in popularity of this diet, which stands for "Calories in Calories Out," is due in large part to enthusiastic posts on social media sites by people who have lost weight with this regimen.
   II. The Plan: This is a do-it-yourself, customized diet, which requires you to first determine how many calories you need to maintain your weight and then subtract 500 calories per day for every pound of weight you would like to lose in a week.
   III. Eating fewer calories than you burn in order to lose weight is not only a time-honored approach but also the basis for the CICO diet.
   IV. The Claim: You can eat what you want and still lose weight as long as you burn more calories than you ingest.
   V. But is it really the optimal way to lose weight?
   The CORRECT answer is:
   A. III, I, V, IV, II   B. I, V, IV, III, II   C. II, I, III, IV, V   D. V, IV, II, III, I

11.____

12.
   I. An even more ambitious fantasy for cybernetics is the production of a fully autonomous life form, something akin to the robots often features in popular science fiction offerings.
   II. If the artificial organ can sense the environment around itself and act accordingly, it need only be attache4d to the appropriate part of the body for its correct functioning.
   III. Such an artificial life form with learning and deductive powers would be able to operate in areas inhospitable to human life.
   IV. If a structure, such as an organ, can take care of its own functioning, then it need not be plugged into the human nervous system, which is a very difficult operation.
   V. A potential use of cybernetics is one much loved by science fiction authors, the replacement of ailing body parts with artificial structures and systems.
   The CORRECT answer is:
   A. I, III, V, IV, II   B. II, I, III, V, IV   C. V, IV, II, I, III   D. IV, II, I, III, V

12.____

13.
   I. The programs can scan documents, enter numbers into spreadsheets, check the accuracy of customer records and make payments with a few automated computer keystrokes.
   II. New software is automating mundane office tasks in operations like accounting, billing, payments, and customer service.

13.____

5 (#1)

III. The technology is still in its infancy, but it will get better, learning as it goes.
IV. The bots are mainly observing, following simple rules and making yes-no decisions, not making higher-level choices that require judgment and experience.
V. So far, often in pilot projects focused on menial tasks, artificial intelligence is freeing workers from drudgery far more often than it is eliminating jobs.
The CORRECT answer is:
A. IV, II, I, III, V   B. II, I, III, V, IV   C. I, III, V, IV, II   D. III, V, IV, II, I

14. I. But the results were often not very good: images of a computer-generated face tended to be blurry or have errors like missing ears.
II. The plan Goodfellow's friends were proposing was to use a complex statistical analysis of the elements that make up a photograph to help machines come up with images by themselves.
III. Researchers were already using neural networks, algorithms loosely modeled on the web of neurons in the human brain, as "generative" models to create plausible new data of their own.
IV. One night in 2014, Ian Goodfellow went drinking to celebrate with a fellow doctoral student who had just graduated.
V. At Les 3 Brasseurs (The Three Brewers), a favorite Montreal watering hole, some friends asked for his help with a thorny project they were working on: a computer that could create photos by itself.
The CORRECT answer is:
A. IV, V, III, I, II   B. V, I, II, IV, III   C. III, II, V, I, IV   D. I, IV, III, II, V

14._____

15. I. Along with working in harmony with other hormones, it regulates the level of blood sugar (glucose).
II. Insulin is a hormone secreted by the pancreas gland, one of the glands in the endocrine system.
III. An insufficient level of insulin secretion leads to high blood sugar, a disease called diabetes mellitus or, simply, diabetes.
IV. Endocrine glands are ductless glands; that is, they pour their products (hormones) directly into the bloodstream.
V. The pancreas, a gland in the upper abdomen, has cells within it that secrete insulin directly into the bloodstream.
The CORRECT answer is:
A. III, I, V, II, IV   B. V, I, III, IV, II   C. IV, II, V, I, III   D. II, I, IV, V, III

15._____

16. I. Since increasing levels of pregnancy hormones cause gestational diabetes, it develops late in pregnancy when pregnancy hormones are at their highest levels.
II. Often, women with gestational diabetes have few symptoms.
III. However, leaving gestational diabetes undiagnosed and untreated is risky to the mother and the developing fetus.
IV. Left untreated, the mother's blood glucose levels will remain consistently high, and these same high levels will occur in the blood of the fetus.
V. The fetal pancreas responds to the high level glucose by secreting large amounts of insulin.

16._____

The CORRECT answer is:
A. IV, III, I, II, V   B. III, IV, V, II, I   C. V, I, IV, II, III   D. I, II, V, IV, III

17. I. Obesity is a condition where the bodies of mammals, such as humans, have stored so much natural energy reserves that the fatty tissues they are stored in have expanded to a point where it is medically considered a significant health risk, with a possible increased rate of mortality to that body.
II. Obesity is also considered generally as any weight that is at least 20 percent above a person's ideal weight.
III. This statistic is further broken down by percentage and degree of obesity: 20 to 40 percent over ideal weight is considered mildly obese, 40 to 100 percent over ideal weight is considered moderately obese, and more than 100 percent over ideal weight is severely (morbidly) obese.
IV. In order to fit the definition of obesity, the excess weight must be due to adipose, or fat, tissue.
V. Muscle mass does not account for the weight attributed to obesity.
The CORRECT answer is:
A. I, II, V, IV, III   B. V, II, III, I, IV   C. IV, I, V, III, IV   D. III, II, I, V, IV

17._____

18. I. Michael Faraday was one of the greatest scientists of the 19th century.
II. His early life closely paralleled that of Benjamin Franklin.
III. His father, a blacksmith, could not afford a formal education for Michael, and so the boy received just the bare essentials and was apprenticed to a bookbinder.
IV. Both were part of a large family; both were apprenticed in the printing trade; both read voraciously and became self-educated; and both loved science.
V. Faraday was born in Newington, Surrey, England, on September 22, 1791.
The CORRECT answer is:
A. I, II, IV, V, III   B. II, IV, V, III, I   C. IV, V, III, I, II   D. V, III, I, II, IV

18._____

19. I. In terms of prestige, however, the Nobel Prizes rank among the highest awards given in each of the six fields.
II. An additional award, the Sveriges Risksbank Prize in Economic Sciences, has also been created independently of the five prizes funded by the Nobel bequest.
III. Nobel Prizes are awarded annually for outstanding contributions in the field of chemistry, literature, peace, physics, and physiology or medicine.
IV. They are funded by a bequest in the will of Alfred B. Nobel, a Swedish inventor.
V. The Nobel Prizes in physics and chemistry and the prize in economics are awarded by the Royal Swedish Academy of Sciences; the literature prize is awarded by the Swedish Academy; the prize in physiology or medicine is given by the Nobel Assembly at the Karolinska Institute; ;and the peace prize is awarded by the Norwegian Nobel Committee.
The CORRECT answer is:
A. V, III, II, I, IV   B. I, V, II, IV, III   C. IV, I, II, III, V   D. III, IV, II, V, I

19._____

20. I. The condition is usually passed on genetically, and is more common in men than in women.
    II. About 7 percent of all men and about 0.6 percent of women inherit the condition.
    III. There is no treatment for color blindness.
    IV. The condition known as color blindness is a defect in vision that causes problems in distinguishing between certain colors.
    V. Individuals can also acquire the condition through various eye diseases.
    The CORRECT answer is:
    A. II, III, I, V, IV   B. IV, I, II, V, III   C. I, II, V, III, IV   D. III, II, IV, V, I

20.____

21. I. In the late 1800s, during the earliest days of photography, however, color photographs required hand painting the color on black-and-white prints.
    II. However, processes such as Lippmann's were cumbersome and required the use of poisonous chemicals such as mercury.
    III. A few decades later, in 1908, physicist and inventory Gabriel Lippmann won the Nobel Prize in physics "for his method of reproducing colors photographically based on the phenomenon of interference."
    IV. His successors began to explore the creation of color photographs using different methods, such as filters.
    V. Today taking color photographs is as easy as picking up a cellphone and snapping a picture.
    The CORRECT answer is:
    A. I, II, III, IV, V   B. V, I, III, II, IV   C. I, II, V, III, IV   D. II, IV, V, I, III

21.____

22. I. Stress is mental, emotional, or physical tension brought about by internal or external pressures such as anxiety or overwork.
    II. Researchers have found significant biochemical changes that take place in the body during stress.
    III. These include elevated blood pressure, depression, cardiovascular disease, stroke, and cancer.
    IV. Thus, stress is a negative way that a person frequently responds to environmental demands or pressures.
    V. Exaggerated, prolonged, or genetic tendencies to stress cause destructive changes which lower the body's immune system response and can lead to a variety of diseases and disorders.
    The CORRECT answer is:
    A. V, IV, III, II, I   B. IV, III, I, II, V   C. I, V, III, II, IV   D. I, IV, II, V, III

22.____

23. I. These fall into two main categories: addictive and non-addictive.
    II. Analgesia, the loss of pain without the loss of consciousness, is of primary importance for the treatment of injury or illness.
    III. Non-addictive analgesics are generally used for treating moderate to severe pain and can be purchased without a prescription as over-the-counter drugs.
    IV. The main agents for accomplishing analgesia in medical practice are analgesic drugs.
    V. More powerful analgesics have the potential for addiction and other undesirable side effects.

23.____

A. II, IV, I, III, V   B. I, V, II, III, IV   C. III, II, V, IV, I   D. IV, V, III, I, II

24.
I. Freshwater makes up less than 3 percent of the world water supply.
II. In 2010, a study published in the science journal Nature predicted that 3.4 billion people are currently vulnerable to freshwater supply shortages.
III. Freshwater is chemically defined as containing a concentration of less than two parts per thousand (<0.2 percent) of dissolved salts (salts that are in solution).
IV. Although water is abundant on the surface of the Earth, freshwater is a very limited resource.
V. The Center for Strategic and International Studies estimate that predicted increases in the world's population will result in a 10 to 20 perce4nt increase in the demand for freshwater each decade.
The CORRECT answer is:
A. I, II, III, V, IV   B. IV, V, I, III, II   C. III, IV, I, II, V   D. II, IV, I, V, III

24.____

25.
I. The relative affordability and pliability of plastic make it a popular material among manufacturers, contributing to the wide availability of products containing plastic.
II. Polyethylene, the most commonly used plastic, did not become available for commercial use in the United States until the end of World War II.
III. Technical advances have led to the creation of different types of polyethylene with unique properties and characteristics that make it suitable for producing a variety of goods.
IV. Polyethylene can be found in packing materials, toys, bulletproof vests, carpet, gold balls, automobile parts, and many other products.
V. Following British chemist Alexander Parkes' introduction to the public of his synthetic plastic compound Parkesine at the 1862 London International Exhibition, plastics have become widely used in consumer goods and their packaging.
The CORRECT answer is:
A. II, I, V, IV, III   B. V, II, III, IV, I   C. I, III, V, II, IV   D. III, V, II, I, IV

25.____

KEY (CORRECT ANSWERS)

1.	C		11.	A
2.	B		12.	C
3.	A		13.	B
4.	D		14.	A
5.	A		15.	D
6.	C		16.	C
7.	B		17.	C
8.	D		18.	A
9.	D		19.	D
10.	B		20.	B

21. B
22. D
23. A
24. C
25. B

TEST 2

DIRECTIONS: The sentences listed below are part of a meaningful paragraph, but they are not given in their proper order. You are to decide what would be the BEST order to put sentences to form a well-organized paragraph. Each sentence has a place in the paragraph; there are no extra sentences. *PRINT THE LETTER OF THE CORRECT ANSWER IN THE SPACE AT THE RIGHT.*

1. I. Imagine all of that—and you have grasped the amount of food the world wastes every year.
    II. Imagine a land mass greater than China.
    III. Then suppose all the crops and produce from those 2.5 billion acres not eaten.
    IV. This level of waste is clearly not acceptable and the case for action becomes even stronger when we consider that 1 in 9 people are malnourished worldwide.
    V. Now imagine that land is only used to produce food.
    The CORRECT answer is:
      A. I, III, IV, II, V   B. II, V, III, I, IV   C. III, V, II, IV, I   D. V, IV, I, III, II

2. I. These totems are part of the city's multimillion-dollar campaign to cut down on greenhouse gas emissions and reliance on landfills, and to turn food scraps and yard waste into compost and, soon, clean energy.
    II. Now, the city is employing the primal chemistry of decay.
    III. Back in the 19th century, the city had a simple method for dealing with organic rubbish by enlisting scavenging swine to nose through the gutters for leftover.
    IV. But now brown bins for organic waste are starting to appear all over the city.
    V. New Yorkers already have blue and green bins for recycling glass, metal, paper, and plastic.
    The CORRECT answer is:
      A. I, V, III, IV, II   B. II, IV, III, V, I   C. IV, II, V, I, III   D. V, IV, I, III, II

3. I. Higher education, also known as postsecondary education, is an optional, advanced level of formal study available to students who have completed the primary (elementary) and secondary (high school) stages of education.
    II. For decades, higher education has been widely viewed as a worthwhile investment for students who wish to increase their future earnings potential.
    III. Although the traditional four-year bachelor's degree is the most recognizable form of postsecondary education in the United States, the term also encompasses master's and doctoral programs, two-year associate degrees, and vocational or career training leading to professional certifications.
    IV. Government officials at the state and federal levels have promoted post-secondary study as a way to build an educated workforce to help the United States compete in a technology-driven global economy.

V. In the twenty-first century, however, skyrocketing tuition costs and student loan debt has raised questions about the utility of higher education and created challenges for policymakers as well as college administrators.
The CORRECT answer is:
A. V, I, IV III, II   B. II, V, I, IV, III   C. I, III, II, IV, V   D. III, II, V, I, IV

4. I. House Democrats this week are expected to unveil a sweeping plan to make college more affordable by reducing debt and simplifying financial aid.
    II. The Democrats' plan would also endeavor to boost graduation rates.
    III. The proposal counters a Republican bill that aims to overhaul the law that dictates the federal government's role in higher education.
    IV. The Higher Education Act, originally passed in 1965, is supposed to be renewed every five years but was last reauthorized a decade ago.
    V. The debate has been closely watched, with members of both parties agreeing that college costs impose an enormous burden on students and families.
    The CORRECT answer is:
    A. III, V, I, IV, II   B. V, I, IV, II, III   C. IV, II, III, V, I   D. II, V, IV, I, III

4.____

5. I. Registration is used to compile lists of eligible voters and is a prerequisite to voting in forty-nine of the fifty states.
    II. In the United States, voter registration is a near-universal feature of the democratic process.
    III. North Dakota is the lone state that does not require it.
    IV. Before an eligible individual can vote in a federal, state, or local election, he or she must register with the relevant authorities, usually at the county or municipal level.
    V. Instead, North Dakota permits residents to simply present valid identification at polling stations.
    The CORRECT answer is:
    A. I, V, II, IV, III   B. III, I, IV, V, I   C. V, II, III, I, IV   D. II, IV, I, III, V

5.____

6. I. However, to increase the size of its forces during extraordinary times, the U.S. military has enacted policies of involuntary recruitment, commonly referred to as conscription, in which citizens are selected for military service through a government draft.
    II. Military recruitment has been voluntary throughout most of the history of the United States armed forces.
    III. While the military has functioned as an all-volunteer force (AVF) since 1973, all males between the ages of eighteen and twenty-five who live in the United States must register with the Selective Service System (SSS), a database of men eligible for potential military conscription should the need arise.
    IV. This requirement is not limited to citizens; only males with current nonimmigrant visas are exempt from registration.
    V. Involuntary military recruitment was used during the Civil War from 1863 to 1865, during World War I from 1917 to 1918, and for an extended period of time from 1940 to 1973.

6.____

The CORRECT answer is:
A. II, I, V, III, IV   B. I, III, IV, II, V   C. V, III, IV, I, II   D. IV, V, II, I, III

7. I. These apparent security fears are a red herring.
    II. As retired Army Lt. Col. Margaret Stock—who had a major role in implementing MAVNI—points out, extreme vetting should be done if there is a specific reason for concern, but not as a general rule for people in a certain class who were born in another country or may have relatives living or working there.
    III. Reportedly, the Pentagon wants to end the program because it claims it does not have the resources necessary to do the enhanced screening or vetting necessary to ensure that these men and women do not pose a security risk to the U.S.
    IV. As a result of MAVNI, more than 10,000 immigrants have joined the Army.
    V. There is no evidence that foreign-born soldiers pose more of a risk to our security than those volunteers born in the U.S.
    The CORRECT answer is:
    A. V, III, II, I, IV   B. IV, III, I, V, II   C. I, V, II, IV, III   D. IV, V, I, II, III

7.____

8. I. Though early computer scientists began tinkering with electronic amusements earlier in the twentieth century, video games became more commonplace beginning in the 1970s with the introduction of the first coin-operated video arcade game Computer Space in 1971.
    II. One year later, the electronics company Magnavox introduced the first home video game console, the Magnavox Odyssey.
    III. During the same period, handheld gaming devices also became more prevalent, making video games a familiar accessory for people on the go.
    IV. The rise of the internet in the 1990s enabled players to connect with other players around the world.
    V. Over the next several decades, both personal computers on which games could be played and in-home video game consoles, including notable machines developed by Atari Nintendo, Sega, Sony, and Microsoft, became increasingly common in U.S. households.
    The CORRECT answer is:
    A. III, IV, I, II, V   B. V, III, IV, I, II   C. I, II, V, III, IV   D. II, I, V, IV, III

8.____

9. I. In the eastern Pacific and Atlantic Oceans, these storms are called hurricanes; in the western Pacific, they are called typhoons; and in the Indian Ocean, they are called cyclones. Other local names also exist.
    II. Under certain conditions, these storm systems will become tropical depressions and then strengthen into tropical storms and become hurricanes when winds exceed speeds.
    III. The names for tropical cyclones vary, depending on which part of the world they are formed.
    IV. These destructive forces form in a series of stages, beginning as systems of strong thunderstorms.
    V. Hurricanes are intense rotating (cyclonic) storms that form over warm tropical waters.

9.____

The CORRECT answer is:
A. I, IV, II, V, III B. V, III, I, IV, II C. V, I, IV, II, III D. II, IV, I, III, V

10. I. Wetlands provide important habitat for a wide variety of plants and animals.
    II. The vegetation of wetlands is adapted to survival under flooded conditions.
    III. Wetlands are low-lying ecosystems that are permanently or periodically saturated with water at or close to the surface.
    IV. However, wetlands are rapidly disappearing because they are being drained and infilled for agricultural, urbanization, and industrial purposes.
    V. The most common types of wetlands are swamps, marshes, shallow open waters, and mires (which contains peat-accumulating fens and bogs).
    The CORRECT answer is:
    A. II, III, V, I, IV B. I, IV, III, V, II C. III, II, V, I, IV D. IV, V, I, II, III

10.____

11. I. Salt marshes are highly productive ecosystems along coastal wetlands that are regularly flooded and drained by tides of salt or brackish water.
    II. They also serve as sites of water filtration, absorbing and converting many pollutants from land runoff, thus potentially avoiding excess nutrient levels in open water than ca spur deadly algal blooms.
    III. The soils are described as porous, soft, and spongy, and are generally filled with grass roots.
    IV. Saturated soils exist in deep muddy layers mixed with peat (decomposing plant matter) and other organic debris that may be several feet deep.
    V. These marshes help prevent shoreline erosion by providing a physical barrier to wave action and by trapping sediments before they flow into open waters.
    The CORRECT answer is:
    A. IV, V, II, I, III B. III, IV, I, II, V C. V, I, III, II, IV D. I, IV, III, V, II

11.____

12. I. They hatch, releasing tiny translucent crustaceans known as fairy shrimp.
    II. Larger creatures—wood frogs, blue-spotted salamanders—lay their eggs in the secluded pools, where no predatory fish might make a meal of them.
    III. It's springtime in the Maine wood and melting snow soaks the forest floor.
    IV. Rain spills off pale new leaves into growing puddles.
    V. Tiny egg cases that endured the winter hidden in the leaf litter begin to thaw out in the water and sun.
    The CORRECT answer is:
    A. III, IV, V, I, II B. I, V, II, III, IV C. V, IV, I, III, II D. I, III, V, II, IV

12.____

13. I. With this in mind, the Celts honored the start of winter with a festival called Samhain (pronounced sow-in).
    II. This occasion merited attention, as the end of summer signaled to the agrarian Celts that now was the time to harvest their crops and begin safeguarding their livestock for the cold winter ahead.
    III. They believed that on this date, the spirits of the past year's dead finally journeyed to the afterlife, but not before wandering the earth to cause mischief among the living.

13.____

IV. During the Iron Age of about 1200 BC to 1 BC, the Gaelic-speaking Celtic people of Britain, Wales, Ireland, Scotland, and other areas of Western Europe marked the first day of the year and the beginning of winter on a date coinciding with the modern November 1.
V. However, the season change also meant something more to the Celts, as the similarities between winter's dark desolation and their human life cycles were not lost on them.
The CORRECT answer is:
  A. IV, II, V, I, III   B. V, III, I, II, IV   C. I, V, II, IV, III   D. V, IV, II, III, I

14. I. Depictions of Halloween and Halloween-themed stories and characters have become commonplace across various forms of media.
II. The festive night has also been the subject of numerous television specials.
III. Halloween occupies a major place in modern popular culture.
IV. Some of the most popular of these include *It's the Great Pumpkin, Charlie Brown* (1966) and The Simpsons' annual "*Treehouse of Horror*" episodes.
V. A wide variety of feature films have been based on Halloween, including *Hocus Pocus* (1993), *Halloweentown* (1998), and director John Carpenter's horror classic *Halloween* (1978).
The CORRECT answer is:
  A. II, IV, III, IV, I   B. III, I, V, II, IV   C. V, III, I, IV, II   D. IV, I, II, V, III

15. I. Many people feared the nations would start a nuclear war, but in the end, a diplomatic solution was reached.
II. The Cuban Missile Crisis was a thirteen-day confrontation between the United States and the Soviet Union in October 1962.
III. The crisis began when the United States discovered the Soviets had been placing nuclear missiles in Cuba—just ninety miles off the coast of Florida.
IV. The Soviets dismantled the missiles and the United States agreed not to invade Cuba.
The CORRECT answer is:
  A. III, II, IV, I   B. I, IV, III, II   C. I, II, IV, III   D. II, III, I, IV

16. I. Ancient Egypt was one of the earlies civilizations in human history.
II. It developed thousands of years ago along the Nile River in northern Africa.
III. Over many centuries, the Ancient Egyptians developed a rich culture that was reflected in their religion, art, and architecture.
IV. The history of Ancient Egypt is often divided into periods categorized by the civilization's political stability and ruling families, or dynasties.
V. Dynastic rule in Ancient Egypt encompassed several thousand years, lasting from about 3100 BC to 30 BC.
The CORRECT answer is:
  A. II, III, V, I, IV   B. III, II, V, IV, I   C. V, I, IV, II, III   D. I, IV, II, III, V

17. I. Like zoos, aquariums feature creatures except that they are home to fish, water animals, and plants.
II. Modern zoos have many other functions, however, including teaching visitors about different habitats and establishing breeding programs to increase the population of species on the verge of extinction.

III. Aquariums are also more than just tourist attractions.
IV. Zoos are places where animals live in captivity and are often on display for the public to see.
V. They help sick and injured fish and animals recover and then return them to the wild.

The CORRECT answer is:
A. V, I, III, IV, II   B. IV, II, I, III, V   C. I, II, IV, V, III   D. II, IV, III, V, I

18. I. The modern Olympic movement was born in 1894 when, at a congress on international sport in Paris, France academic Pierre de Coubertin organized the first International Olympic Committee, and proposed that the first modern Olympic games be held in Athens, Greece, in 1896.
II. It had been almost 1,500 years since the ancient Greek games had been banned by the Roman emperors.
III. In the 18th and 19th centuries, several regional and national sporting events were held, modeled on the Olympic games of ancient Greece.
IV. (At the same conference, organizers also agreed to hold the second games at Paris in 1900.)
V. None of the sporting events would grow to become the ongoing tradition represented by today's Olympic movement.

The CORRECT answer is:
A. V, I, III, IV, II   B. IV, I, III, II, V   C. I, IV, II, III, V   D. II, I, IV, V, III

19. I. The idea of communism had been circulating throughout Europe, particularly in France, since the early 1940s.
II. In 1848, Karl Marx, a German-born political theorist, provided the foundation for modern communist theory in his famous manuscript, *The Manifesto of the Communist Party* (known more widely as *The Communist Manifesto* and co-written by his longtime colleague, Friedrich Engels).
III. Marx built upon these ideas, developing his own theory regarding the forces of history (historical materialism), the inevitability of class struggle and revolution, and the specific conditions under which a society might transition from capitalism to socialism and then to pure communism.
IV. Although the word possibly dates as far back as eighteenth-century French, it was not until the mid-nineteenth century that a theory of communism, and the evolution of economic and social reform that it entailed began to spread throughout Europe.
V. Communism is a political and economic doctrine, the aim of which is to abolish private ownership of property and for-profit enterprise and to replace these with public ownership and control of industry, agriculture, and natural resources.

The CORRECT answer is:
A. V, IV II, I, III   B. III, I, II, IV, V   C. I, IV, III, V, II   D. II, I, V, III, IV

20.
   I. McCarthy and his allies claimed that communists had infiltrated the federal government and other institutions, and were threatening the American way of life.
   II. During the late 1940s and early 1950s, U.S. Senator Joseph McCarthy, a Wisconsin Republican, led a tidal wave of anti-communist political repression in the United States.
   III. Originally associated with generic Cold War anticommunism, the term McCarthyism eventually came to refer to a particularly mean-spirited and groundless accusation based on paranoia and characterized by political grandstanding.
   IV. The attacks were often baseless, but they nevertheless destroyed the careers of thousands of individuals.
   V. Often these individuals had done nothing more than attend a left-wing political meeting ten or fifteen years earlier.
   The CORRECT answer is:
   A. I, II, IV, V, III   B. III, II, I, IV, V   C. V, III, II, I, IV   D. II, I, IV, V, III

21.
   I. John Edgar, known simply as Edgar for most of his life, was their fourth child.
   II. Fifteen years older, his brother had arrived first, followed by two sisters.
   III. Devoutly religious, his mother, Annie M. Scheitlin, ruled the family with a strict hand.
   IV. J. Edgar Hoover was born on January 1, 1895, in the still-struggling town of Washington, D.C.
   V. His father, Dickerson Hoover, Sr., held a minor government position, chief of printing for the geodetic survey department.
   The CORRECT answer is:
   A. V, III, IV, I, II   B. I, V, II, III, IV   C. IV, III, V, I, II   D. III, I, II, IV, V

22.
   I. The most well-known instances of impeachment have involved the office of the president. However, other officials, such as federal judges, can also be impeached.
   II. These checks and balances help ensure no branch becomes too powerful.
   III. The United States Constitution includes checks and balances on each branch of government.
   IV. One of the checks and balances described in the Constitution is impeachment.
   V. The Constitution indicates that any federal official, up to and including the president, can be impeached.
   The CORRECT answer is:
   A. III, II, IV, V, I   B. II, V, III, I, IV   C. IV, III, I, II, V   D. V, I, II, IV, III

23.
   I. A recession is a downturn in the economy.
   II. For practical purposes, however, most economists agree that a recession is best defined more loosely as an extended period of decreased economic activity marked by a number of characteristics.
   III. Those characteristics include the following: high unemployment rates, a decline in the profits made by corporations, and a decrease in the amount of money people are investing in the stock market.

IV. Economists have two ways of identifying when a recession is occurring.
V. According to the most precise definition, a recession is a decline in a country's gross domestic product, or GDP (the total value of all goods and services produced within that country in a specific time period), for two or more successive quarters (in the financial world, each year is commonly broken down into four three-month periods called quarters).

The CORRECT answer is:
   A. IV, III, I, V, II   B. I, IV, V, II, III   C. II, III, I, IV, V   D. III, IV, II, I, V

24.
I. Book bans can be issued by a variety of authorities.
II. Governments of religious institutions are often the ones who initiate large-scale book bans.
III. On the other hand, small-scale book bans are commonly enacted by minor governing bodies, such as school boards, at the urging of groups of concerned individuals.
IV. The stated reasons for the banning of specific books often vary depending on the body initiating the ban in question.
V. For example, a government may ban books that express views contrary to those of the state or that are seen as being in some way threatening to the welfare of the state.

The CORRECT answer is:
   A. I, V, III, II, IV   B. V, II, I, IV, III   C. II, IV, III, V, I   D. IV, III, V, I, II

25.
I. April Fools' Day, also known as All Fools' Day, is an informal holiday observed annually on April 1 with pranks, practical jokes, and hoaxes.
II. The purpose of this is to mock playfully those who have been deceived.
III. The origin of this "holiday" is not known, but historians believe it may have originated in late sixteenth-century France, when the French government adopted the Gregorian calendar.
IV. This change left some citizens observing New Year's Day on April 1 instead of January 1, and these people were ridiculed as fools.
V. The tradition of playing jokes on unsuspecting people on April 1 expanded around the world over the centuries.

The CORRECT answer is:
   A. I, II, III, V, IV   B. V, IV, I, II, III   C. III, I, V, II, IV   D. IV, III, II, I, V

KEY (CORRECT ANSWERS)

1.	B	11.	D
2.	D	12.	A
3.	C	13.	A
4.	A	14.	B
5.	D	15.	D
6.	A	16.	C
7.	B	17.	B
8.	C	18.	C
9.	B	19.	A
10.	C	20.	D

21.	C
22.	A
23.	B
24.	D
25.	B

www.ingramcontent.com/pod-product-compliance
Lightning Source LLC
Chambersburg PA
CBHW082123230426
43671CB00015B/2791